T0365293

Cambridge Elements ☰

Elements in Non-Local Data Interactions: Foundations and Applications
edited by
Luca Calatroni
Centre National de la Recherche Scientifique (CNRS)

A PROLEGOMENON TO DIFFERENTIAL EQUATIONS AND VARIATIONAL METHODS ON GRAPHS

Yves van Gennip
Delft University of Technology

Jeremy Budd
University of Birmingham

CAMBRIDGE
UNIVERSITY PRESS

Shaftesbury Road, Cambridge CB2 8EA, United Kingdom

One Liberty Plaza, 20th Floor, New York, NY 10006, USA

477 Williamstown Road, Port Melbourne, VIC 3207, Australia

314–321, 3rd Floor, Plot 3, Splendor Forum, Jasola District Centre,
New Delhi – 110025, India

103 Penang Road, #05–06/07, Visioncrest Commercial, Singapore 238467

Cambridge University Press is part of Cambridge University Press & Assessment,
a department of the University of Cambridge.

We share the University's mission to contribute to society through the pursuit of
education, learning and research at the highest international levels of excellence.

www.cambridge.org
Information on this title: www.cambridge.org/9781009494656

DOI: 10.1017/9781009346641

First published 2025

A catalogue record for this publication is available from the British Library.

ISBN 978-1-009-49465-6 Hardback
ISBN 978-1-009-34663-4 Paperback
ISSN 2755-1296 (online)
ISSN 2755-1288 (print)

A Prolegomenon to Differential Equations and Variational Methods on Graphs

Elements in Non-Local Data Interactions: Foundations and Applications

DOI: 10.1017/9781009346641
First published online: February 2025

Yves van Gennip
Delft University of Technology
Jeremy Budd
University of Birmingham

Author for correspondence: Yves van Gennip, Y.vanGennip@tudelft.nl

Abstract: The study of differential equations on graphs emerged about 15 years ago as a way of providing a framework for the mathematical analysis of images. Since then it has burgeoned and has expanded more broadly to encompass image processing and, more recently, machine learning. The authors have provided a bird's-eye view of both theoretical developments and concrete applications that will enable newcomers to quickly get a flavour of key results. Additionally, they provide an exhaustive, at the time of writing, bibliography which will point readers to where fuller details and other directions can be explored. This title is also available as open access on Cambridge Core.

Keywords: differential equations on graphs, variational methods on graphs, machine learning, image analysis, image processing

ISBNs: 9781009494656 (HB), 9781009346634 (PB), 9781009346641 (OC)
ISSNs: 2755-1296 (online), 2755-1288 (print)

Contents

1 Introduction

The Element you are about to read tells a tale that shrank in the writing. The opposite is true for its companion volume [190]. When we were asked to write a contribution to what would become the Elements in Non-local Data Interactions: Foundations and Applications series in April 2021,[1] quickly the idea took hold to provide an overview, a snapshot of the field of differential equations and variational methods on graphs and their applications to machine learning, image processing, and image analysis. But this is a very active field, being developed in a variety of different directions, and so the story we wanted to tell outgrew the format of a contribution to the Cambridge Elements series. We are grateful to Cambridge University Press and the editors for deeming our full contribution worthy enough of its own publication [190] and allowing us to extract and adapt some introductory sections for publication in the Elements series. This Element provides an introduction to differential equations and variational methods on graphs seen through the lenses of the authors. It focuses on some areas to which we ourselves have actively contributed, but at the same time aims to give sufficient background to equip the interested reader to explore this fascinating topic. We have aimed to make this Element a satisfyingly comprehensive read in itself, while also allowing it to be a teaser for its more extensive companion volume. Those who compare both volumes will find that the companion volume contains, besides additional details in some of the sections that correspond to those in the current Element, chapters on applications of differential equations on graphs and their computational implementation, as well as chapters on further theoretical explorations of the relationships between various graph-based models and of the continuum limits of such models when the number of nodes of the underlying graph is taken to infinity.

Differential equations, both ordinary differential equations (ODEs) and partial differential equations (PDEs), have a long history in mathematics and we assume they need no introduction to the reader. Slightly younger, yet still of a venerable age, is the study of graphs.[2] By a differential equation on a graph

---

[1] The idea for this Element and its companion book owes a great debt to the Nonlocal Methods for Arbitrary Data Sources (NoMADS) project funded by the European Union's Horizon 2020 research and innovation programme (Marie Skłodowska-Curie grant agreement No. 777826).

[2] In this Element, by 'graph' we mean the discrete objects consisting of vertices and (potentially weighted) edges connecting the vertices that are studied in graph theory. Where we want to talk about the graph of a function, this is made explicit. As is quite common, we tend to use 'graph' and 'network' [78] interchangeably, although some might prefer to distinguish between networks in the real world and the mathematical graphs that can be used to model them. We also use related terminology, such as vertices and nodes [15, box 2.1], interchangeably.

we mean a discretization of a differential equation, usually a PDE, on a graph: if we can write the PDE as $F(u(x,t)) = 0$, for a differential operator F and a function u defined on (a subset of) $\mathbb{R}^m \times \mathbb{R}$, then we obtain a differential equation[3] on a graph by replacing the (spatial) derivatives with respect to x in F by finite difference operators based on the structure of the graph and replacing u by a function defined on (a subset of) $V \times \mathbb{R}$, where V is the set of nodes of the graph.

Variational models in the calculus of variations are typically formulated in terms of minimization of a function(al). To consider such a model on a graph, we discretize the functional by replacing integrals with the appropriate sums and differential operators with the corresponding finite difference operators on graphs. This process also turns finite-dimensional the space of admissible functions over which the functional is minimized. The line between calculus of variations and mathematical optimization becomes blurry here, or is even crossed. Because the authors of this Element approach these models from the point of view of variational calculus, we will include them under the umbrella of variational models (on graphs), even if the originators of any particular model may have had a different inspiration when proposing that model.

The field of machine learning is concerned with the development of methods and algorithms to analyse data sets. 'Learning' in this context refers to leveraging the properties of some collection of 'training data' (which may or may not be a part of the data set which is to be analysed) to draw conclusions about the data set. Machine learning has undertaken an enormous flight in the twenty-first century. Terms like 'big data', 'machine learning', and 'artificial intelligence' are now commonplace for many people, both because of the commercial successes of the many tech companies that exist by the grace of data availability and the methods to learn from the data, and because of the enormous speed with which deep-learned algorithms have transformed many areas of science, industry, and public and private life. Scientific curiosity goes hand in hand with a societal need to understand the methods that play such a big role in so many sectors.

But what is the role of differential equations in all of this? After all, many of the advances in machine learning, both in terms of development of new methods and analysis of existing ones, come from statistics, computer science, and the specific application fields – scientific or industrial – where the methods are used. One might argue for the general notion that increased diversity in the points of view from which a particular topic is scrutinized leads to different and complementary insights that all strengthen the full picture. There certainly

---

[3] Or a difference equation, if u does not depend on the variable t.

is validity in that notion when it comes to the study of machine learning; in this case, though, there are stronger ties that go beyond generalities.

A substantial part of the root system of differential equations in machine learning lies in the field(s) of mathematical image processing and image analysis.[4] Not only do (the ingredients of) many differential-equation-based machine learning methods have roots in the mathematical imaging literature and many machine learning methods have applications in imaging problems, but there is also a substantial overlap in the communities active in these fields.

Despite the success of artificial neural networks, they are not central objects in this Element. The main focus in the current Element is on those methods that represent the data (e.g., the image) in terms of a graph in order to apply a graph-based variational model or differential equation.

These methods have many desirable properties, which have made them popular in recent years. Because the graph-based models and equations have close connections to well-established models and equations in the continuum setting, there is a wealth of ideas to pursue and techniques to apply to study and understand them. Moreover, the development of numerical methods for differential equations has a long and rich history, yielding many algorithms that can be adapted to the graph-based setting. Another key difference between most machine learning methods discussed in this Element compared to deep learning methods is that the latter are mostly data-driven,[5] which usually means many training data are required to obtain well-performing networks, while the former are explicitly model-driven and so tend to require fewer training data (but also are less likely to discover patterns for which the models are not built to look).

The scope of this Element is broad in some parts and narrow in others. On the one hand, we wish to provide an overview of an exciting, ever-broadening, and expansive field. Thus, in the general literature overview in Section 2 we have taken a very broad view of the topic of differential equations on graphs and their applications with the aim of placing it in its historical context and pointing the reader to the many aspects and fields that are closely related to it. On the other hand, in the remainder of this Element, we focus on very specific models with a certain amount of bias in the direction of those models with which the authors have close experience themselves, yet not to the complete exclusion of other models. These models revolve around the graph Ginzburg–Landau functional,

---

[4] We sometimes refer to these two fields collectively as 'imaging' or 'mathematical imaging', or just 'image analysis' for brevity.

[5] Although there are recent trends to incorporate (physical) models into the data-driven machinery.

which is introduced in this Element in Section 5 and which plays a central role in a number of graph-based clustering and classification methods.

Graph clustering and classification are similar tasks that both aim to use the structure of the graph to group its nodes into subsets called clusters or classes (or sometimes communities or phases, depending on the context or application). In most of the settings that we discuss here, these subsets are required to be pairwise disjoint, so that mathematically we can speak of a partition of the node set (assuming nonempty subsets) and we obtain non-overlapping clusters or classes. A key guiding principle of both tasks is to have strong connections (i.e., many edges or, in an edge-weighted graph, highly weighted edges) between nodes in the same class or cluster and few between nodes in different clusters or classes.[6] This is not the only requirement for a good clustering or classification – in the absence of any other desiderata, a trivial partition of the node set into one cluster would maximize intra-cluster connectivity and minimize inter-cluster connectivity – and so additional demands are typically imposed. Two types of constraints that will receive close attention in this Element are constraints on cluster sizes and constraints that encourage fidelity to a priori known class membership of certain nodes. The presence of such a priori known labels is what sets classification apart from clustering.

There are mathematical imaging tasks that can be formulated in terms of graph clustering or classification, most notably image segmentation, which can be viewed as the task of clustering or classifying the pixels of a digital image based on their contribution to (or membership of) objects of interest in the image. Other imaging tasks, such as image denoising, reconstruction, or inpainting, can be formulated in ways that are mathematically quite closely related to graph clustering and classification.

We hope this Element may serve as an overview and an inspiration, both for those who already work in the area of differential equations on graphs and for those who do not (yet) and wish to familiarize themselves with a field rich with mathematical challenges and abundant applications.

1.1 Outline of This Element

We give a brief overview of the history of and literature in the field of differential equations and variational methods on graphs with applications in machine learning and image analysis in Section 2. For a more extensive overview, we refer to section 1.2 of the companion volume [190]. In Section 3 we lay the

---

[6] There may be deviations from or additions to this general requirement. For example, in Macgregor and Sun [135] (see also Macgregor [133, chapter 6]) the goal is to find two clusters (with an algorithm that is local, in the sense that its run time is independent of the size of the graph) that are densely connected to each other, but weakly to the rest of the graph.

mathematical foundations that we require to formulate differential equations and variational models on graphs. For example, we define spaces of node functions and important operators and functionals on these spaces, such as the graph Laplacian operators and the graph total variation functional.

In most of this Element we consider undirected graphs, but in Section 4 we discuss very briefly works that generalize some of the concepts from Section 3 to directed graphs, in particular graph Laplacians.

Besides the graph total variation functional, another very important graph-based functional, which we have already mentioned, is the graph Ginzburg–Landau functional. It deserves its own place in the spotlight; thus, in Section 5 we introduce it and discuss some of its variants and properties, including its connection to the graph total variation functional.

The spectrum of an operator gives insight into its behaviour. In Section 6 indeed we see that the spectra of graph Laplacians shed some light on their usefulness in graph clustering and classification problems.

The role of functionals in variational models is as 'energy' or an 'objective function' that needs to be minimized. Two important dynamical systems that (approximately) accomplish this minimization for the graph Ginzburg–Landau functional are described by the graph Allen–Cahn equation and the graph Merriman–Bence–Osher scheme, respectively. The former, which is an ordinary differential equation obtained as a gradient flow of the graph Ginzburg–Landau functional, is the topic of Section 7, while the latter is the focus of Section 8.

Closely related to the graph Allen–Cahn and Merriman–Bence–Osher dynamics are the graph mean curvature flow dynamics that are described in Section 9. Although exactly how closely these are related is still an open question, one property most of them have in common is a threshold on the parameter of the model below which the dynamics trivializes. This freezing phenomenon is discussed in Section 10.

The main focus in this Element is on models that cluster or classify the node set of the graph into two subsets. In Section 11 we take a look at multiclass extensions of some of these models.

In Section 12 we discuss some finite difference methods on graphs, namely Laplacian learning and Poisson learning. Finally, Section 13 provides a brief conclusion to this Element as we look forward (or sideways) to additional topics that appear in the companion volume [190].

2 History and Literature Overview

Any area of mathematical enquiry will have its roots in what came before. The field of differential equations on graphs for clustering and classification problems is no exception, so there is always the risk that the starting point of any historical overview may feel somewhat arbitrary. It is inescapably personal too; the priorities and narratives generated by our own research inevitably have influenced our departure point for this story and the route we will follow afterwards. As such, the references given in this section are not meant to be exhaustive, nor are all contributions from the references that are given always exhaustively described. One reason this field has generated such enthusiastic interest is that it brings together ideas from many different directions, from statistics and machine learning to discrete mathematics and mathematical analysis. We encourage any attempts to understand the history of this field from perspectives different from the one we provide here, shining more light on the exciting diversity of viewpoints differential equations on graphs have to offer.

For a fuller overview of the literature, we refer to section 1.2 of the companion volume [190]. Neither the current section nor the literature section in the companion volume are exhaustive overviews, if such a thing is even a possibility, but they should provide enough starting points for someone who is eager to learn about this active field of research. We apologize for the undoubtedly many important works in their respective areas that are missing from our bibliography.

As a double ignition point for the growing interest in differential equations on graphs by the (applied) mathematical analysis community in the late noughties and early tens of the twenty-first century, especially in relation to image processing and data analysis applications, we mention works by Abderrahim Elmoataz and collaborators such as [63, 75, 131] – which have a strong focus on p-Laplacians, ∞-Laplacians, and morphological operations such as dilation and erosion on graphs, as well as processing of point clouds in three dimensions – and works by Andrea L. Bertozzi and collaborators, like [21, 22, 144, 189, 191] – which deal with the Ginzburg–Landau functional on graphs and derived dynamics such as the Allen–Cahn equation and Merriman–Bence–Osher (MBO) scheme on graphs. This is not to say there were no earlier investigations into the topic of differential operators and equations on graphs, for example in [160, 195] or in the context of consensus problems [150, 164], or variational 'energy' minimization problems on graphs, such as in the context of Markov random fields [181], but the two groups we mentioned earlier provided a sustained drive for the investigation of both the applied and theoretical aspects of differential equations on graphs in the setting on which we are focusing in the current Element.

We note that in the current Element, when we talk about *differential equations on graphs*, we typically mean partial differential equations whose spatial derivatives have been replaced by discrete finite difference operators on graphs (see Section 3.2), leading to ODEs or finite-difference equations. A priori this is different from the systems of PDEs formulated on the edges of a network that are coupled through boundary conditions on the nodes, which are also studied under the name 'differential equations on graphs (or networks)' [192].

New research directions tend not to spring into being fully formed, and also the works mentioned earlier have had the benefit of a rich pre-existing literature in related fields. In particular, many of the variational models and differential equations that are studied on graphs have been inspired by continuum cousins that came before and by the, often sizeable, literature that exists about those models and equations. Examples are the Allen–Cahn equation [5], the Cahn–Hilliard equation [40], the Merriman–Bence–Osher scheme [146, 147], flow by mean curvature [6, 30, 167], total variation flow [9], and the Mumford–Shah and Chan–Vese variational models [47, 159].

Inspiration has also come from other directions, such as discrete calculus [101] and numerical analysis and scientific computing [18]. The latter fields not only provide state-of-the-art methods that allow for fast implementations of the graph methods on graphs with many nodes – something which is very import-ant in modern-day applications that deal with large data sets or high-resolution images – but also offer theoretical tools for dealing with discretizations of con-tinuum equations, even though the specifics may differ substantially between a discretization designed with the goal of approximating a continuum problem as accurately as possible and a discretization which is a priori determined by the graph structure that is given by the problem or inherent in the application at hand.

Some of the most prominent applications that have been tackled by differ-ential equations and variational models on graphs, especially by the models and methods central to the current Element, are graph clustering and classifica-tion [174], and other applications that are – or can be formulated to become – related, such as community detection [171], image segmentation [46], and graph learning [200]. For an extensive look at these, and other, applications, we refer to chapter 4 of the companion volume [190]. In the current Element we focus on the core graph clustering and classification applications.

Since the early pioneering works we mentioned at the start of this section, differential equations on graphs have enjoyed a lot of attention from applied analysts and researchers from adjacent fields. As a very rough attempt at clas-sification of these different research efforts, we distinguish between those papers that study differential equations and variational models purely at the discrete-graph level and those that are interested in continuum limits of those discrete equations and models as a way to establish their *consistency*. (Some papers may combine elements of both categories.) The focus of this Element is on the first category. For a closer look at the second category, we refer to chapter 7 of [190].

In this first category, we encounter papers that study particular graph-based differential operators or graph-based dynamics, such as the eikonal equation (and the related eikonal depth), p-eikonal equation, p- and ∞-Laplacians [38, 42, 76, 138, 206], semigroup evolution equations [153], dynamics [121] such as mean curvature flow and morphological evolution equations (related to morphological filtering and graph-based front propagation) [70, 182] or advection [172], or discrete variational models such as trend filtering on graphs [194] and the graph Mumford–Shah model [106, 168].

Of special interest in the context of the current Element are the graph Allen–Cahn equation, graph MBO scheme, and graph mean curvature flow [33, 144, 187, 191], which are discussed in much greater detail in Sections 7, 8, and 9. For details about applications in which these graph-based dynamics have been used, we refer to chapter 4 of [190]. Some of the applications that are considered in that volume require an extension of the classical two-phase versions of the Allen–Cahn and MBO dynamics to a multiclass context [94, 95]; other variations on multiclass MBO have been developed, such as an incremental reseeding method [31] and auction dynamics [110].

The publications focusing on the discrete level also include papers that study connections between graph-based differential operators or dynamics on the one hand, and on the other hand graph-based concepts that are useful for studying graph structures, which sometimes already had a history outside of the differential-equations-on-graphs literature. For example: the modulus on graphs [3], Cheeger cuts and ratio cuts [141], ranking algorithms and centrality measures such as heat kernel PageRank [142], nonconservative alpha-centrality (as opposed to conservative PageRank) [98], centrality measures and community structure based on the interplay between dynamics via parameterized (or generalized) Laplacians and the network structure [201], random walks and SimRank on uncertain graphs (i.e., graphs in which each edge has a probability of existence assigned to it) [209], distance and proximity measures on graphs [12, 48], and a hubs-biased resistance distance (based on graph Laplacians) [79].

We also draw attention here to graph-based active learning [148], Laplacian learning [211], Poisson learning [44], and results on the Lipschitz regularity of functions in terms of Laplacians on point clouds [45]. For overview articles about graph-based methods in machine learning and image processing, we refer to [20, 23, 51].

In the continuum setting, the dynamics of both the Allen–Cahn equation and the MBO scheme are known to approximate flow by mean curvature, in a sense that has been made precise through convergence analysis [16, 32, 39, 80, 125, 126]. Rigorous connections between the graph Allen–Cahn equation and graph MBO scheme have been established in [33, 35, 36, 37]; their connections with graph mean curvature flow are open questions. Details about these established connections and open questions, as well as a closer look at the various dynamics in the continuum setting, can be found in chapter 6 of [190].

In many of the works just cited, the graphs under consideration on which the variational models or differential equations are formulated are finite, undirected graphs, with edges that connect nodes pairwise and that, if weighted, have a positive weight. Moreover, the graphs are unchanging – also, for the continuum limits that we briefly mentioned, even though the limit $|V| \to \infty$ is considered, typically at each fixed $|V|$, the graph structure is static.

This leaves a lot of room for generalizations and extensions. In this Element we refrain from delving into these generalizations in too much detail, although in Section 4 we do briefly discuss Laplacians on directed graphs [17, 87, 104, 207]. Other possible generalizations are to multislice networks [151], hypergraphs (in which edges can connect more than two nodes) [26, 108], metric graphs and quantum graphs (in which edges are represented by intervals of the real line) [118], signed graphs that can have positive and negative edge weights [60], metric random walk spaces (of which locally finite positively edge-weighted connected graphs are a special case) [139, 140][7], and graphs changing in time [25].

Of interest also is the connection between methods on graphs and the constructions used to build the graphs, as is considered in, for example, [97]. Some more details about building graph models for specific applications are given in section 4.2 of [190].

3 Calculus on Undirected Edge-Weighted Graphs

3.1 Graphs, Function Spaces, Inner Products, and Norms

Except where explicitly stated otherwise, in this Element we consider finite,[8] simple (i.e., without multi-edges[9] and without self-loops[10]), connected,[11] edge-weighted graphs $G = (V, E, \omega)$ – if a graph G is mentioned without further

---

[7] In [139] heat flow on metric random walk spaces is studied, in [140] total variation flow.

[8] This means $|V| < \infty$.

[9] Given two nodes $i, j \in V$, there is at most one edge $(i, j) \in E$, as is already implied by $E \subseteq V \times V$.

[10] Each edge connects two distinct nodes, that is, for all $i \in V$, $(i, i) \in (V \times V \setminus E)$. For a preprint discussing Laplacians (which we will introduce later) on graphs with self-loops see Açıkmeşe [2].

[11] The definition of connectivity is given later in this section.

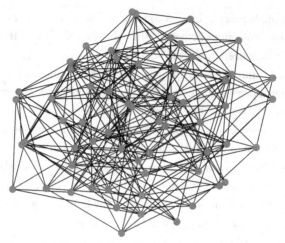

Figure 3.1 An example of a finite, simple, connected, and undirected graph.

specification, it is assumed to have these properties. Figure 3.1 shows an example of such a graph. Here V is the set of nodes or vertices of the graph, $E \subseteq V \times V$ is the set of edges,[12] and $\omega \colon V \times V \to \mathbb{R}$ is the edge weight function which vanishes on $E^c := (V \times V) \setminus E$; thus $\omega|_{E^c} = 0$. Unless otherwise specified, we assume that $\omega|_E > 0$. In this framework, an unweighted graph $G = (V, E)$ can be viewed as an edge-weighted graph $G = (V, E, \omega)$ with $\omega|_E = 1$.

We will assume that $|V| \geq 2$. It will often be useful to identify the nodes in V with the numbers 1 to $n \in \mathbb{N}$,[13] and we write $V = [n] := \{1, 2, \ldots, n\}$. Unspecified nodes from V we denote by $i, j, k, \ldots$. The edge from i to j is denoted by (i, j); the nodes i and j are endpoints of this edge. For any node function u, that is, a function u whose domain is (a subset of) V, we write u_i for $u(i)$. Similarly, for any function φ whose domain is (a subset of) $V \times V$, we write φ_{ij} for $\varphi(i, j)$. Any such function which vanishes on E^c we will call an edge function. We define the function spaces of node and edge functions,

$$\mathcal{V} := \{u \colon V \to \mathbb{R}\}, \qquad \mathcal{E} := \{\varphi \colon V \times V \to \mathbb{R} \colon \varphi|_{E^c} = 0\}.$$

We use subscripts to indicate alternative codomains: if A is a set, then

$$\mathcal{V}_A := \{u \colon V \to A\}, \qquad \mathcal{E}_A := \{\varphi \colon V \times V \to A \colon \varphi|_{E^c} = 0\}.$$

In particular, $\mathcal{V} = \mathcal{V}_{\mathbb{R}}$ and $\mathcal{E} = \mathcal{E}_{\mathbb{R}}$.

---

[12] In this particular case, since we do not allow self-loops, E is always a strict subset of $V \times V$.

[13] To avoid ambiguity, we note that we write $\mathbb{N}$ for the strictly positive natural numbers and $\mathbb{N}_0 := \mathbb{N} \cup \{0\}$. Also, to avoid ambiguity regarding zero, we call the numbers in the sets $(0, \infty)$ and $(-\infty, 0)$ strictly positive and strictly negative, respectively.

When it is not explicitly stated differently (as in Section 4), we consider undirected graphs, namely graphs for which $(i, j) \in E$ if and only if $(j, i) \in E$. Two nodes $i, j \in V$ in an undirected graph are called adjacent, or neighbours, if $(i, j) \in E$. The condition that $j \neq i$, which is sometimes explicitly included in the definition of neighbour, is superfluous under our assumption of absence of self-loops. The matrix A with entries $A_{ij} := \omega_{ij}$ is called the (weighted) adjacency matrix, or weight matrix of the graph. In an undirected graph, we require ω to be symmetric in its arguments, that is, for all $i, j \in V$, $\omega_{ij} = \omega_{ji}$. Some authors demand their edge functions $\varphi \in \mathcal{E}$ to be skew-symmetric, namely $\varphi_{ij} = -\varphi_{ji}$. We do not require this assumption and so will not impose it.

Since we consider graphs without self-loops, for all $i \in V$, $\omega_{ii} = 0$. The degree of node i is $d_i := \sum_{j \in V} \omega_{ij}$. A graph is connected if, for all $i, j \in V$ with $i \neq j$, there exist finitely many nodes $i_1, i_2, \ldots, i_k$ such that $i_1 = i$, $i_k = j$, and $\omega_{i_1 i_2} \cdots \omega_{i_{k-1} i_k} > 0$. A graph which is not connected is called disconnected. Since our graphs are assumed to be connected (unless stated otherwise), we have, for all $i \in V$, $d_i > 0$.

In some situations it will be useful to have a shorthand notation to indicate adjacency of nodes (in an undirected graph): for $i \in V$, we write $j \sim i$ if and only if $j \in V$ and $(i, j) \in E$. Equivalently under our assumption that $\omega|_E > 0$, we have that $j \sim i$ if and only if $j \in V$ and $\omega_{ij} > 0$.

Our first step to defining a calculus on node and edge functions is to define an inner product structure[14] on $\mathcal{V}$ and $\mathcal{E}$. Let[15] $r \in [0, 1]$, $q \in [1/2, 1]$ (see Remark 3.9), $u, v \in \mathcal{V}$, and $\varphi, \psi \in \mathcal{E}$. Then

$$\langle u, v \rangle_{\mathcal{V}} := \sum_{i \in V} d_i^r u_i v_i \quad \text{and} \quad \langle \varphi, \psi \rangle_{\mathcal{E}} := \frac{1}{2} \sum_{(i,j) \in E} \omega_{ij}^{2q-1} \varphi_{ij} \psi_{ij}. \tag{3.1}$$

We note that the factor $\frac{1}{2}$ compensates for the 'double count' of edges (i, j) and (j, i) in an undirected graph. In this and other circumstances it can be convenient to rewrite the sum over $(i, j) \in E$ as a double sum over $i, j \in V$. This can be done since $\varphi_{ij} = \psi_{ij} = \omega_{ij} = 0$ if $(i, j) \notin E$. In this case we have to interpret ω_{ij}^0 to be 0 (not 1!) if $(i, j) \notin E$.

---

[14] At first glance it may seem that the bilinear forms defined here are not inner products, since $\langle u, u \rangle_{\mathcal{V}}$ may be zero, even if $u \neq 0$, if there is an $i \in V$ such that $d_i^r = 0$, and similarly $\langle \varphi, \varphi \rangle_{\mathcal{E}}$ may be zero, even if $\varphi \neq 0$, if there are $i, j \in V$ such that $\omega_{ij}^{2q-1} = 0$. However, the possibility $d_i^r = 0$ is excluded by our assumption of connectedness and, while $\omega_{ij}^{2q-1} = 0$ will be true for some $i, j \in V$ for all graphs except complete graphs, the definition of $\mathcal{E}$ requires $\varphi_{ij} = 0$ for such i and j.

[15] The intervals $[0, 1]$ and $[1/2, 1]$ from which r and q are chosen, respectively, are mostly intervals of convenience: they cover the most common values that appear in the literature – $r \in \{0, 1\}$ and $q \in \{1/2, 1\}$ – and allow for interpolation between them. We do not expect major, or possibly any, changes to be necessary if we allow $r, q \in \mathbb{R}$ instead.

These inner products induce norms in the usual way: $\|u\|_\mathcal{V} := \sqrt{\langle u, u \rangle_\mathcal{V}}$ and $\|\varphi\|_\mathcal{E} := \sqrt{\langle \varphi, \varphi \rangle_\mathcal{E}}$. Other commonly used norms on $\mathcal{V}$ and $\mathcal{E}$ are the p-norms (for $p \in [1, \infty)$) and ∞-norms:

$$\|u\|_{\mathcal{V},p} := \left(\sum_{i \in V} d_i^r |u_i|^p \right)^{\frac{1}{p}}, \qquad \|\varphi\|_{\mathcal{E},p} := \left(\frac{1}{2} \sum_{i,j \in V} \omega_{ij}^{2q-1} |\varphi_{ij}|^p \right)^{\frac{1}{p}},$$

$$\|u\|_{\mathcal{V},\infty} := \max\{|u_i| : i \in V\}, \qquad \|\varphi\|_{\mathcal{E},\infty} := \max\{|\varphi_{ij}| : i,j \in V\}.$$

We note that the $p = 2$ norms are the norms induced by the inner products.

If $r = 0$, then $\|u\|_\mathcal{V}$ is the Euclidean 2-norm of the vector with components u_i. To avoid specifying $r = 0$, we may write $\|u\|_2$ in this case, with ℓ^2 inner product $\langle \cdot, \cdot \rangle_2$. We also use this notation for vectors not (necessarily) meant to be interpreted as node functions. Similarly, if $r = 0$, then $\|u\|_{\mathcal{V},p}$ is equal to the p-norm for the vector with components u_i and we may write $\|u\|_p$ instead.

If $S \subseteq V$, we define χ_S to be its indicator (or characteristic) function, that is,

$$(\chi_S)_i := \begin{cases} 1, & \text{if } i \in S, \\ 0, & \text{if } i \in S^c := V \setminus S. \end{cases}$$

In particular $\chi_V = 1 \in \mathcal{V}$ (and we may write 1 for χ_V, or c for $c\chi_V$, if $c \in \mathbb{R}$ is a constant) and $\chi_\emptyset = 0 \in \mathcal{V}$. Similarly, we define indicator functions $\chi_{E'}$ for edge subsets $E' \subseteq E$. We will also need a variant indicator function ι_A for $A \subseteq \mathbb{R}$, defined to be $\iota_A(x) = 0$ if $x \in A$ and $\iota_A(x) = +\infty$ if $x \in \mathbb{R} \setminus A$.

The volume of a node subset $S \subseteq V$ and volume of an edge subset $E' \subseteq E$ are defined to be (for any $p \in [1, \infty)$), respectively,

$$\text{vol}(S) := \|\chi_S\|_{\mathcal{V},p}^p = \sum_{i \in S} d_i^r, \quad \text{vol}(E') := \|\chi_{E'}\|_{\mathcal{E},p}^p = \frac{1}{2} \sum_{(i,j) \in E'} \omega_{ij}^{2q-1}. \quad (3.2)$$

Lemma 3.1. *In this lemma we interpret $\frac{1}{\infty} = 0$. Let $u, v \in \mathcal{V}$ and $\varphi, \psi \in \mathcal{E}$. For all $p, p' \in [1, \infty]$ such that $\frac{1}{p} + \frac{1}{p'} = 1$, these Hölder inequalities hold:*

$$\|uv\|_{\mathcal{V},1} \le \|u\|_{\mathcal{V},p} \|v\|_{\mathcal{V},p'} \quad \text{and} \quad \|\varphi\psi\|_{\mathcal{E},1} \le \|\varphi\|_{\mathcal{E},p} \|\psi\|_{\mathcal{E},p'}.$$

Moreover, these embedding estimates are satisfied, if $s, t \in [1, \infty]$ with $s \le t$:

$$\|u\|_{\mathcal{V},s} \le (\text{vol}(V))^{\frac{1}{s} - \frac{1}{t}} \|u\|_{\mathcal{V},t} \quad \text{and} \quad \|\varphi\|_{\mathcal{E},s} \le (\text{vol}(E))^{\frac{1}{s} - \frac{1}{t}} \|\varphi\|_{\mathcal{E},t}.$$

Furthermore,

$$\lim_{p \to \infty} \|u\|_{\mathcal{V},p} = \|u\|_{\mathcal{V},\infty} \quad \text{and} \quad \lim_{p \to \infty} \|\varphi\|_{\mathcal{E},p} = \|\varphi\|_{\mathcal{E},\infty}.$$

In fact, for all $p \in [1, \infty)$ we have

$$\min_{i \in V} d_i^{\frac{r}{p}} \|u\|_{\mathcal{V},\infty} \le \|u\|_{\mathcal{V},p} \le (\text{vol}(V))^{\frac{1}{p}} \|u\|_{\mathcal{V},\infty}$$

and

$$2^{-\frac{1}{p}} \min_{(i,j)\in E} \omega_{ij}^{\frac{2q-1}{p}} \|\varphi\|_{\mathcal{E},\infty} \le \|\varphi\|_{\mathcal{E},p} \le (\mathrm{vol}\,(E))^{\frac{1}{p}} \|\varphi\|_{\mathcal{E},\infty}.$$

Proof. For a proof we refer to lemma 2.1.1 of [190]. □

Instead of interpreting $\varphi \in \mathcal{E}$ in the standard way as a function from $V \times V$ to $\mathbb{R}$, we may also view it as a function from V to $\mathcal{V}$: for all $i \in V$, $\varphi_i. \in \mathcal{V}$. This prompts the following definitions of a node-dependent inner product and p- and ∞-norms: for all $\varphi, \psi \in \mathcal{E}$, all $i \in V$, and all $p \in [1, \infty)$,

$$(\varphi, \psi)_i := \frac{1}{2} \sum_{j\in V} \omega_{ij}^{2q-1} \varphi_{ij}\psi_{ij},$$

$$\|\varphi\|_{i,p} := \left(\frac{1}{2} \sum_{j\in V} \omega_{ij}^{2q-1} |\varphi_{ij}|^p \right)^{\frac{1}{p}}, \tag{3.3}$$

$$\|\varphi\|_{i,\infty} := \max\{|\varphi_{ij}| : j \in V\}.$$

Corollary 3.2. *In this corollary we interpret $\frac{1}{\infty} = 0$. Let $\varphi, \psi \in \mathcal{E}$ and $i \in V$. For $p, p' \in [1, \infty]$ such that $\frac{1}{p} + \frac{1}{p'} = 1$, a Hölder inequality holds:*

$$\|\varphi\psi\|_{i,1} \le \|\varphi\|_{i,p} \|\psi\|_{i,p'}.$$

Moreover, an embedding estimate is satisfied, if $s, t \in [1, \infty]$ with $s \le t$:

$$\|\varphi\|_{i,s} \le \left(\frac{1}{2} \sum_{j\in V} \omega_{ij}^{2q-1} \right)^{\frac{1}{s}-\frac{1}{t}} \|\varphi\|_{i,t}.$$

Furthermore, for all $\varphi \in \mathcal{E}$ and for all $p \in [1, \infty)$,

$$2^{-\frac{1}{p}} \min_{\substack{j\in V \\ \omega_{ij}>0}} \omega_{ij}^{\frac{2q-1}{p}} \|\varphi\|_{i,\infty} \le \|\varphi\|_{i,p} \le \left(\frac{1}{2} \sum_{j\in V} \omega_{ij}^{2q-1} \right)^{\frac{1}{p}} \|\varphi\|_{i,\infty},$$

and thus in particular,

$$\lim_{p\to\infty} \|\varphi\|_{i,p} = \|\varphi\|_{i,\infty}.$$

Proof. We refer to corollary 2.1.2 in [190]. □

3.2 Graph Gradient, (p-)Dirichlet Energy, (p-)Laplacian, and Total Variation

To be able to do calculus on graphs, we require a discrete analogue of the derivative: the graph gradient. For $u \in V$ the gradient $\nabla u \in \mathcal{E}$ is defined by[16]

$$(\nabla u)_{ij} := \omega_{ij}^{1-q}(u_j - u_i).$$

Remark 3.3. The graph gradient provides a good motivation for defining the node-dependent inner product and norms in (3.3). The continuum gradient ∇u of a function $u : \mathbb{R}^m \to \mathbb{R}$ is a vector-valued function with length $\|\nabla u\|_2$ – or, in general, p-norm – a real-valued function on $\mathbb{R}^m$. Analogously, in the graph setting the node-dependent norms from (3.3) are real-valued functions on V.

In Ta *et al.* [183] a connection is made between the node-dependent ∞-norms and morphological dilation and erosion operators, if $q = 1$ or $\omega(V \times V) \subseteq \{0, 1\}$. Using superscripts $+$ and $-$ to denote the positive part $x^+ := \max(0, x)$ and negative part $x^- := -\min(0, x)$ of a number $x \in \mathbb{R}$, respectively, we compute

$$\|(\nabla u)^+\|_{i,\infty} = \max_{j \sim i} \max(0, u_j - u_i)$$

$$= \max\{u_j : j = i \text{ or } j \sim i\} - u_i =: (\delta_a(u))_i - u_i,$$

$$\|(\nabla u)^-\|_{i,\infty} = \max_{j \sim i}(-\min(0, u_j - u_i)) = -\left[\min\{u_j : j = i \text{ or } j \sim i\} - u_i\right]$$

$$= u_i - \min\{u_j : j = i \text{ or } j \sim i\} =: u_i - (\varepsilon_a(u))_i.$$

In [183] the operators δ_a and ε_a are called the dilation and erosion operators, respectively, in analogy to similar operators in the continuum setting. We can understand these names, if we apply the operators to the indicator function $u = \chi_S$ of a node subset $S \subseteq V$. Then $\delta_a(u) = \chi_{S^\delta}$ and $\varepsilon_a(u) = \chi_{S^\varepsilon}$, where the dilated set S^δ consists of S with all the nodes that have at least one neighbour in S added, and the eroded set S^ε consists of S with all the nodes that have at least one neighbour in S^c (i.e., $V \setminus S$) removed. In El Chakik *et al.* [70] on weighted graphs the nonlocal dilation operator and nonlocal erosion operator,

$$(\text{NLD}(u))_i := u_i + \|(\nabla u)^+\|_{i,\infty} \quad \text{and} \quad (\text{NLE}(u))_i := u_i - \|(\nabla u)^-\|_{i,\infty},$$

respectively, are introduced. The preceding computation shows that in the case of an unweighted graph, $\delta_a = \text{NLD}$ and $\varepsilon_a = \text{NLE}$.

We define the graph divergence $\text{div} : \mathcal{E} \to V$ to be given by

$$(\text{div } \varphi)_i := \frac{1}{2} d_i^{-r} \sum_{j \in V} \omega_{ij}^q (\varphi_{ji} - \varphi_{ij}),$$

---

[16] Recall the convention that $\omega_{ij}^0 = 0$ if $\omega_{ij} = 0$.

since this is the adjoint of the graph gradient: it can be checked that, for all $u \in \mathcal{V}$ and all $\varphi \in \mathcal{E}$, $\langle \nabla u, \varphi \rangle_{\mathcal{E}} = \langle u, \operatorname{div} \varphi \rangle_{\mathcal{V}}$. We thus define a graph Laplacian[17] $\Delta \colon \mathcal{V} \to \mathcal{V}$ as the divergence of the gradient:

$$(\Delta u)_i := (\operatorname{div} \nabla u)_i = d_i^{-r} \sum_{j \in V} \omega_{ij}(u_i - u_j). \tag{3.4}$$

We note that Δ is independent of q. If $r = 0$, Δ is called the combinatorial (or unnormalized) graph Laplacian, while if $r = 1$, it is called the random walk (or asymmetrically normalized) graph Laplacian. We note that Δ is self-adjoint:

$$\langle u, \Delta v \rangle_{\mathcal{V}} = \langle \Delta u, v \rangle_{\mathcal{V}}. \tag{3.5}$$

Remark 3.4. Since we consider finite graphs with $|V| = [n]$, there is a bijective correspondence between functions in $u \in \mathcal{V}$ and (column) vectors in $\mathbb{R}^n$ with entries u_i. It follows that linear operators on $\mathcal{V}$ can be represented by matrices. In particular, the graph Laplacian Δ has associated matrix $D^{-r}(D - A) = D^{1-r} - D^{-r}A$, where D is the diagonal degree matrix with $D_{ii} := d_i$ and, as in Section 3.1, the matrix A is the weighted adjacency matrix with entries $A_{ij} = \omega_{ij}$. In particular, the matrix associated to the combinatorial graph Laplacian is $D - A$, and to the random walk graph Laplacian[18] is $I - D^{-1}A$, where by I we denote the identity matrix of the appropriate size. To avoid complicating the notation and text, we will freely use both kinds of representation without always explicitly noting any switches or changing notation; for example, u can denote a function or vector and Δ may be the Laplacian operator or matrix. We note that the multiplication of two node functions uv becomes a matrix-vector multiplication Uv in vector notation, with U the diagonal matrix with $U_{ii} = u_i$.

Remark 3.5. The name random walk Laplacian for Δ with $r = 1$ comes from the fact that the $D^{-1}A$ term in the associated matrix $I - D^{-1}A$ (see Remark 3.4) is a right-stochastic matrix, that is, its rows sum to one, and can thus be interpreted as the transition matrix of a discrete-time Markov chain with $(D^{-1}A)_{ij} = d_i^{-1}\omega_{ij}$ being the probability of the transition from state i to state j in a single time step. Associating the states with nodes of a graph, the Markov chain describes a random walk on that graph. The (negative) unnormalized graph Laplacian

---

[17] These graph Laplacians can also be defined in terms of an incidence matrix of the graph, i.e., a matrix that has nonzero entry in the ith row and kth column, if and only if node i is an endpoint of edge k (under some arbitrary, yet fixed, ordering of the edges, where in an undirected graph (i, j) and (j, i) are treated as being a single edge); see for example [55, section 1.2]. We do not explicitly use this characterization of graph Laplacians in this work.

[18] The random walk graph Laplacian is sometimes also called the left-normalized graph Laplacian to distinguish it from the right-normalized graph Laplacian that has associated matrix $I - AD^{-1}$. This latter Laplacian does not fit into the framework of (3.4), but can be represented as member of the two-parameter family of graph Laplacians in (3.7).

$-\Delta$ (with $r = 0$) is the (infinitesimal) generator of a continuous-time Markov chain,[19] as described in detail in remark 2.1.5 in [190].

Remark 3.6. We would be remiss not to mention the symmetrically normalized Laplacian, which is represented in matrix form as

$$\Delta^{\mathrm{sym}} := D^{-\frac{1}{2}}(D-A)D^{-\frac{1}{2}} = D^{r-\frac{1}{2}}(D^{1-r} - D^{-r}A)D^{-\frac{1}{2}} = I - D^{-\frac{1}{2}}AD^{-\frac{1}{2}}. \quad (3.6)$$

This graph Laplacian appears frequently in the literature, for example, Chung [55], but is not captured in the preceding framework, as it would require a different scaling for each term in the gradient ∇u. We refer to Zhou and Schölkopf [206, section 2.3] for details. We note that Δ^{sym} is self-adjoint, with respect to $\langle \cdot, \cdot \rangle_{\mathcal{V}}$ for $r = 0$. More generally, the two-parameter normalized graph Laplacian

$$\Delta^{(s,t)} := D^{-s}(D-A)D^{-t} \quad (3.7)$$

is self-adjoint with respect to $\langle \cdot, \cdot \rangle_{\mathcal{V}}$ for[20] $r = s - t$. Furthermore, for all $a \in \mathbb{R}$

$$D^{-a}\Delta^{(s,t)}D^a = \Delta^{(s+a,t-a)}$$

and so $\Delta^{(s,t)}$ and $\Delta^{(s',t')}$ are similar whenever $s + t = s' + t'$. In particular, $\Delta^{(s,t)}$ is similar to the symmetric matrix $\Delta^{((s+t)/2,(s+t)/2)}$ and thus Δ and Δ^{sym} are similar when $r = 1$. For further details, we refer to Budd [34, chapter 2].

In Smola and Kondor [180, theorem 3] it is shown that graph Laplacians are, in a sense, invariant to vertex permutations. It is also shown that they are, in some sense, the only linear operators that depend linearly on the graph's adjacency matrix to be so.

In Zhou and Belkin [208] a geometry graph Laplacian is used, defined as

$$L^{\mathrm{geom}} := I - (D^{\mathrm{geom}})^{-1}A^{\mathrm{geom}},$$

where $A^{\mathrm{geom}} := D^{-1}AD^{-1}$ and D^{geom} is the corresponding degree matrix. We also mention that in Merkurjev *et al.* [145] a multiscale Laplacian is introduced.

The graph Dirichlet 'energy' of $u \in \mathcal{V}$ (as defined in e.g. Van Gennip and Bertozzi [189, appendix A]) is

$$\frac{1}{2}\|\nabla u\|_{\mathcal{E}}^2 = \frac{1}{2}\langle u, \Delta u \rangle_{\mathcal{V}} = \frac{1}{4}\sum_{i,j \in V} \omega_{ij}(u_i - u_j)^2$$

$$= \max\{\langle \mathrm{div}\ \varphi, u \rangle_{\mathcal{V}} : \varphi \in \mathcal{E} \text{ and } \|\varphi\|_{\mathcal{E}} \leq 1\}. \quad (3.8)$$

We observe that $\|\nabla u\|_{\mathcal{E}}^2$ does not depend on q.

---

[19] The authors thank Jonas Latz for this observation.

[20] We can allow any $s, t \in \mathbb{R}$, so in this context r is not restricted to $[0, 1]$.

For Poincaré inequalities [61, 66, 81] involving the Dirichlet energy on (infinite) graphs, we refer to [58, 129]. Computing the Gateaux derivative of the Dirichlet energy, we recognize the graph Laplacian:

$$\frac{d}{d\alpha}\frac{1}{2}\|\nabla(u+\alpha v)\|_{\mathcal{E}}^2\bigg|_{\alpha=0} = \frac{1}{2}\frac{d}{d\alpha}\Big[\langle\Delta u,u\rangle_{\mathcal{V}} + 2\alpha\langle\Delta u,v\rangle_{\mathcal{V}} + \alpha^2\langle\Delta v,v\rangle_{\mathcal{V}}\Big]_{\alpha=0}$$

$$= \langle\Delta u,v\rangle_{\mathcal{V}}, \tag{3.9}$$

where $\alpha \in \mathbb{R}$, $u,v \in \mathcal{V}$, and we have used the self-adjointness of Δ from (3.5).

In [34, theorem 4.1.2] it is shown that the two-parameter normalized graph Laplacian from (3.7) also is the first variation of a Dirichlet-type functional:

$$\frac{d}{d\alpha}\frac{1}{2}\|\nabla D^{-t}(u+\alpha v)\|_{\mathcal{E}}^2\bigg|_{\alpha=0} = \langle\Delta^{(s,t)}u,v\rangle_{\mathcal{V}},$$

where $(D^{-t}u)_i = d_i^{-t}u_i$ and in the $\mathcal{V}$-inner product $r = s - t$.

Changing the edge function norm in the maximum formulation in (3.8) to a maximum norm leads to a definition of graph total variation:

$$\mathrm{TV}(u) := \max\{\langle\operatorname{div}\varphi,u\rangle_{\mathcal{V}} : \varphi \in \mathcal{E} \text{ and } \|\varphi\|_{\mathcal{E},\infty} \le 1\}$$

$$= \frac{1}{2}\sum_{i,j\in V}\omega_{ij}^q|u_i - u_j| = \|\nabla u\|_{\mathcal{E},1}. \tag{3.10}$$

The second equality in (3.10) follows since the maximum in the definition is achieved at $\varphi = \operatorname{sgn}(\nabla u)$ (where the signum function acts elementwise: $\varphi_{ij} = \operatorname{sgn}(u_j - u_i)$), where sgn can be any representative of the signum function equivalence class in $L^1_{\mathrm{loc}}(\mathbb{R})$, that is, $\operatorname{sgn}(x) = 1$ if $x > 0$, $\operatorname{sgn}(x) = -1$ if $x < 0$, and $\operatorname{sgn}(0)$ may be defined to equal any arbitrary, but determined, real number.[21] This can be seen by rewriting $\langle\operatorname{div}\varphi,u\rangle_{\mathcal{V}} = \langle\varphi,\nabla u\rangle_{\mathcal{E}}$. This will play a role again when we consider curvature in Section 9. For the final equality in (3.10) we used that the edge weights ω_{ij} are nonnegative.

If $u \in \mathcal{V}_{\{0,1\}}$, then $(u_i - u_j)^2 = |u_i - u_j|$ and thus by (3.8), if $q = 1$, then

$$\|\nabla u\|_{\mathcal{E}}^2 = \frac{1}{2}\sum_{i,j\in V}\omega_{ij}(u_i - u_j)^2 = \frac{1}{2}\sum_{i,j\in V}\omega_{ij}|u_i - u_j| = \mathrm{TV}(u).$$

Analogously to the 'anisotropic' total variation in (3.10), an isotropic total variation can be defined. See Van Gennip *et al.* [191, remark 2.1].

---

[21] The usual definition includes $\operatorname{sgn}(0) = 0$. Some of the works we cite use a different definition at $x = 0$ or do not specify the value in $x = 0$.

The graph p-Dirichlet energy – so called in analogy to the Dirichlet energy in (3.8) – is

$$
\frac{1}{p}\|\nabla u\|_{\mathcal{E},p}^p = \frac{1}{2p}\sum_{i,j\in V}\omega_{ij}^{2q-1}|\omega_{ij}^{1-q}(u_j-u_i)|^p
$$

$$
= \frac{1}{2p}\sum_{i,j\in V}\omega_{ij}^{(2-p)q+p-1}|u_i-u_j|^p. \tag{3.11}
$$

We note that for $p=2$ indeed we recover the graph Dirichlet energy from (3.8) and for $p=1$ we obtain the graph total variation from (3.10).

For $p\in[1,\infty)$, the graph p-Laplacian $\Delta_p\colon V\to V$ is defined[22] via the Gateaux derivative of the p-Dirichlet energy by requiring that, for all $u,v\in V$,

$$
\langle\Delta_p u,v\rangle_V = \frac{d}{ds}\frac{1}{p}\|\nabla(u+sv)\|_{\mathcal{E},p}^p\Big|_{s=0}
$$

$$
= \frac{1}{2}\sum_{i\in V}\sum_{\substack{j\in V\\u_j\neq u_i}}\omega_{ij}^{(2-p)q+p-1}|u_i-u_j|^{p-2}(u_i-u_j)(v_i-v_j)
$$

$$
= \sum_{i\in V}\sum_{\substack{j\in V\\u_i\neq u_j}}\omega_{ij}^{(2-p)q+p-1}|u_i-u_j|^{p-2}(u_i-u_j)v_i. \tag{3.12}
$$

(We note that we used the symmetry of ω.) Thus, for all $u\in V$ and for all $i\in V$,

$$
(\Delta_p u)_i := d_i^{-r}\sum_{\substack{j\in V\\u_j\neq u_i}}\omega_{ij}^{(2-p)q+p-1}|u_i-u_j|^{p-2}(u_i-u_j). \tag{3.13}
$$

From (3.9) we see that we recover our standard graph Laplacian if we choose $p=2$. For other values of p, the operator Δ_p is not linear. We note that (for general p), if $q=1$, then the exponent of ω_{ij} in Δ_p equals 1 (see Remark 3.9).

By splitting the sum in (3.13), we obtain

$$
(\Delta_p u)_i = d_i^{-r}\sum_{\substack{j\in V\\u_i>u_j}}\omega_{ij}^{(2-p)q+p-1}(u_i-u_j)^{p-1} - d_i^{-r}\sum_{\substack{j\in V\\u_j>u_i}}\omega_{ij}^{(2-p)q+p-1}(u_j-u_i)^{p-1}
$$

$$
= 2d_i^{-r}\|\omega^{\frac{1-q}{p}}(\nabla u)^-\|_{i,p-1}^{p-1} - 2d_i^{-r}\|\omega^{\frac{1-q}{p}}(\nabla u)^+\|_{i,p-1}^{p-1}.
$$

In particular, $\Delta_p u=0$ if and only if, for all $i\in V$, $\|\omega^{\frac{1-q}{p}}(\nabla u)^-\|_{i,p-1} = \|\omega^{\frac{1-q}{p}}(\nabla u)^+\|_{i,p-1}$. From the final inequalities in Corollary 3.2, we know that

---

[22] Another graph p-Laplacian does appear in the literature, for example in [75, 76, 206], inspired by the p-Laplacian in the continuum (about which section 3.7.5 in [190] contains some information). For further details we refer to footnote 40 in [190].

$$\lim_{p\to\infty} \|\omega^{\frac{1-q}{p}}(\nabla u)^-\|_{i,p-1} = \|(\nabla u)^-\|_{i,\infty},$$

$$\lim_{p\to\infty} \|\omega^{\frac{1-q}{p}}(\nabla u)^+\|_{i,p-1} = \|(\nabla u)^+\|_{i,\infty}.$$

This inspires the following definition[23] of the graph ∞-Laplacian from Elmoataz *et al.* [73], for all $u \in V$ and for all $i \in V$:

$$(\Delta_\infty u)_i := \|(\nabla u)^-\|_{i,\infty} - \|(\nabla u)^+\|_{i,\infty}.$$

Then $\Delta_\infty u = 0$ if and only if, for all $i \in V$, $\|(\nabla u)^-\|_{i,\infty} = \|(\nabla u)^+\|_{i,\infty}$. The results in Lemma 3.7 give further justification for this definition of Δ_∞. In order to state the lemma, we need the concept of lexicographic ordering of edge functions (we refer to Kyng *et al.* [123, section 2]): given functions $\varphi, \psi \in \mathcal{E}$, we define $\varphi \preceq \psi$ if and only if, after reordering the values of φ and ψ in nonincreasing order, the first value of φ that is different from the corresponding value of ψ is smaller than this corresponding value, or no such value exists (i.e., φ and ψ are equal after the reorderings).

Lemma 3.7. *Let $S \subseteq V$ be a nonempty subset and let $u^0 : S \to \mathbb{R}$. The minimization problem*

$$\operatorname*{argmin}_{u\in V} \|\nabla u\|_{\mathcal{E},\infty} \quad s.t. \quad u|_S = u^0$$

has a solution. Out of all minimizers, there is a unique one u^*, which satisfies, for all $u \in V$ with $u|_S = u^0$, $\nabla u^* \preceq \nabla u$. Moreover, if $u \in V$ with $u|_S = u^0$, then $u = u^*$ if and only if, for all $i \in V \setminus S$, $(\Delta_\infty u)_i = 0$. Furthermore, for $p \in (1,\infty)$, the minimization problem

$$\operatorname*{argmin}_{u\in V} \|\nabla u\|_{\mathcal{E},p} \quad s.t. \quad u|_S = u^0$$

has a unique solution u^p. If $q = \frac{1}{2}$, then $\lim_{p\to\infty} u^p = u^*$.

Proof. We refer to lemma 2.1.7 in [190]. □

Because it is the first variation of the graph p-Dirichlet energy (see (3.12)), the graph p-Laplacian in (3.13) is sometimes also called the

---

[23] The definition of the graph ∞-Laplacian is not fully consistent throughout the literature. Some definitions differ by an overall sign change or an overall factor $\frac{1}{2}$, for example in [72, 74]. In Flores *et al.* [90] it is defined at node i to be $\min_{j\in V}(\nabla u)_{ij} + \min_{j\in V}(\nabla u)_{ij}$ inspired by equation (2.18) in [190]. As we can see in the proof of Lemma 3.7, which is given in lemma 2.1.7 of [190], the solution set of the important equation $(\Delta_\infty u)_i = 0$ is the same under all these definitions. The choice of q in ∇u may also differ between papers, with $q = \frac{1}{2}$ and $q = 1$ being common choices.

variational graph p-Laplacian to distinguish it from the game-theoretic graph p-Laplacian[24]

$$\Delta_p^{\text{game}} := \frac{1}{p}\Delta + \alpha\left(1 - \frac{2}{p}\right)\Delta_\infty, \tag{3.14}$$

for some constant $\alpha > 0$; see Flores *et al.* [90].[25] A similar operator is used in Elmoataz *et al.* [72], where it is called the graph normalized p-Laplacian and where the constants in the linear combination of Δ and Δ_∞ are kept as parameters that can be chosen depending on the application.

For a generalization of the discrete calculus presented in these past few sections to (undirected and directed) hypergraphs, that is, 'graphs' whose (hyper)edge set E is a subset of $\mathcal{P}(V) \setminus \{\emptyset\}$,[26] we refer to [26, 88, 89, 108, 112].

Remark 3.8. Hypergraphs do not receive much attention in this work, but we do want to mention a string of recent works by Mulas, Jost, and collaborators, which define graph Laplacians [112] and p-Laplacians [113] on hypergraphs, study their spectra[27] [92, 155, 157], investigate random walks [156] and other hypergraph dynamics [24], and generalize concepts such as the Cheeger cut [154], independence number (i.e., the maximum size of a subset $S \subseteq V$ such that, for all distinct $i, j \in S$, there is no hyperedge to which they both belong), and colouring number (i.e., the fewest colours needed to colour all vertices such that no hyperedge contains two vertices with the same colour) [1] to hypergraphs.

We note that Mulas *et al.* [155] also provides generalizations of graph Laplacians to signed graphs (which are graphs in which edge weights can be positive and negative), graphs with self-loops, and directed graphs. For the latter case, the graph Laplacian from Bauer [17] is used; see Section 4.

For extensions to hypergraphs of the graph limit theories of graphons and graphops (see chapter 7 of [190]) we refer to Elek and Szegedy [71] and Zhao [203] (hypergraphons), and Zucal [212] (hypergraphops), respectively.

Methods on hypergraphs have been applied to problems related to our interests in this work, for example hypergraph signal processing in Zhang *et al.* [202], heat diffusion on hypergraphs for finding bipartite components in Macgregor and Sun [134] (see also Macgregor [133, chapter 7]), and semi-supervised learning (see section 4.1.2 in [190]) on hypergraphs for early diagnosis of Alzheimer's disease in Aviles-Rivero *et al.* [11].

---

[24] The definition of the game-theoretic graph p-Laplacian is not consistent throughout the literature. For more details we refer to footnote 43 of [190].

[25] See also Peres and Sheffield [170] for the game-theoretic Laplacian in the continuum setting.

[26] Here $\mathcal{P}(V)$ denotes the power set of V, namely, the set of all subsets of V.

[27] We refer to Section 6 for information about the spectrum of (non-hyper)graph Laplacians.

3.3 Miscellaneous Considerations

To define the distance d_{ij}^G between two nodes i and j on a graph G, we first need the concept of a path on V. If $i, j \in V$ are distinct nodes, a path γ_{ij} from i to j is a tuple of $\ell \in \mathbb{N}$ distinct vertices $\gamma_{ij} = (i_1, \ldots, i_\ell)$ such that $i_1 = i$, $i_\ell = j$, and, for all $k \in [\ell - 1]$, $i_{k+1} \sim i_k$. The length of the path γ_{ij} is defined to be

$$|\gamma_{ij}| := \sum_{k=1}^{\ell} \omega_{i_k i_{k+1}}^{q-1}.$$

The reasons for this choice of scaling of ω are explored in some more detail in Remark 3.9. We now define the graph distance between nodes $i \neq j$ as

$$d_{ij}^G := \min_{\gamma_{ij}\,:\ \text{a path from } i \text{ to } j} |\gamma_{ij}|. \tag{3.15}$$

We also define $d_{ii}^G := 0$. We note that the path of minimal length between two neighbouring nodes, is not necessarily the 'direct' path (i, j). If $S \subseteq V$ is not empty, we define the distance from $i \in V$ to S as

$$d_i^S := \min_{j \in S} d_{ij}^G.$$

For $S = \emptyset$ we define, for all $i \in V$, $d_i^\emptyset := +\infty$. By Manfredi *et al.* [138, section 3.1, example 2], if $S \neq \emptyset$, $u = d^S$ is the unique solution to an eikonal equation:

$$\begin{cases} \min_{j \sim i} (\nabla u)_{ij} = -1, & \text{if } i \in V \setminus S, \\ u_i = 0, & \text{if } i \in S. \end{cases}$$

That d^S is a solution can be understood as follows. If $i \in V \setminus S$, the minimum value of $(\nabla d^S)_{ij}$ among all neighbours j of i will be achieved at a j that lies on a shortest path from i to S, in which case $d_j^S - d_i^S = -d_{ij}^G = -\omega_{ij}^{q-1}$ and thus $(\nabla d^S)_{ij} = -1$. If $i \in S$, then $d_i^S = 0$. For a proof of uniqueness we refer to [138, section 6.2]. We note that the eikonal equation, while inspired by a differential equation from the continuum setting, is a difference equation on graphs.

It is useful to note that we can rewrite the eikonal equation. Let $i \in V \setminus S$. Since the equation requires $\min_{j \sim i} (\nabla u)_{ij} = -1$, we can replace ∇u by $-(\nabla u)^-$ without changing the equation. Since $\min_{j \sim i} [-(\nabla u)_{ij}^-] = -\max_{j \sim i} (\nabla u)_{ij}^- = -\|(\nabla u)^-\|_{i,\infty}$, we rewrite the eikonal equation as

$$\begin{cases} \|(\nabla u)^-\|_{i,\infty} = 1, & \text{if } i \in V \setminus S, \\ u_i = 0, & \text{if } i \in S. \end{cases}$$

Remark 3.9. The parameter q, introduced in the definition of the $\mathcal{E}$-inner product and used in the definition of the gradient, does not appear in the Laplacian and Dirichlet energy, but it does impact the definition of total variation.

There are two common choices for q. If we imagine the graph gradient to be a generalization of the finite-difference discretization of the continuum gradient from a regular grid to a general graph, it is natural to associate ω_{ij}^{1-q} with the length scale h^{-1}, where h is the mesh size of the 'grid'. Reasoning similarly for the graph Laplacian, which 'should' be analogous to a finite-difference discretization of the continuum Laplacian, $d_i^{-r}\omega_{ij} = h^{-2}$. If the weights ω_{ij} are scaled by a constant factor, the degree d_i scales with the same factor, thus $\omega_{ij}^{1-r} \propto h^{-2}$. Hence $\omega_{ij}^{1-r}/\omega_{ij}^{1-q} = \omega_{ij}^{q-r} \propto h^{-2}/h^{-1} = h^{-1}$. As both ω_{ij}^{q-r} and ω_{ij}^{1-q} scale with h^{-1}, we might choose q by $q - r = 1 - q$, that is, $q = \frac{1}{2}(1 + r)$. The common picks $r = 0$ and $r = 1$ then correspond to $q = \frac{1}{2}$ and $q = 1$, respectively.

This numerical-analysis-based analogy cannot be extended indefinitely. If we want to interpret the summations in the Dirichlet energy and total variation as discrete quadratures approximating integrals, then the volume of the grid cells of the discretization will have to be incorporated into ω_{ij}. Since this volume depends on the dimension of the space over which it is being integrated, this cannot be made consistent with our preceding considerations.

In the remainder of this work (except in Sections 4, 5.3, and 9 where q returns very briefly) we will make the choice $q = 1$, even when $r \neq 1$. This is inspired by Theorem 5.1, which states that the graph Ginzburg–Landau functional (which we will define in Section 5) Γ-converges to graph total variation *with $q = 1$* in the relevant parameter limit $\varepsilon \downarrow 0$. The graph Ginzburg–Landau functional, which is at the heart of much that is discussed in this Element, is independent of q; the fact that in the limit total variation with $q = 1$ appears can thus be viewed as a selection criterion for our parameter choice.

Another advantage of choosing $q = 1$ is that the exponent of ω_{ij} in the graph p-Dirichlet energy in (3.11) is independent of p (and equal to 1) if and only if $q = 1$. The graph p-Dirichlet energy is a common choice of regularizer in graph-based variational models (see section 12 and section 4.1 in [190]) and gave rise to the graph p-Laplacian in (3.13).

If $G = (V, E)$ is an unweighted graph, we call the graph $G' = (V', E')$ a subgraph of G if $V' \subseteq V$, $E' \subseteq E$, and $(i, j) \in E'$ implies $i, j \in V'$. If, additionally, $i, j \in V'$ and $(i, j) \in E$ implies $(i, j) \in E'$, then G' is called an induced subgraph (or vertex-induced subgraph, or subgraph induced by V') of G. A subgraph G' of G is connected if for all distinct nodes $i, j \in V'$, there exists a path from i to j. A subgraph G' is a component (or connected component) if it is connected and it is maximal in the sense that if G'' is a connected subgraph of G and G' is a subgraph of G'', then $G'' = G'$. Any connected component of G necessarily is an induced subgraph of G.

These notions straightforwardly carry over to the case in which $\tilde{G} = (V, E, \omega)$ is an edge-weighted graph; that is, we call $\tilde{G}' = (V', E', \chi_{E'}\omega|_{V' \times V'})$[28] a subgraph of $\tilde{G}$, a (vertex-)induced subgraph of $\tilde{G}$, connected, or a connected component of $\tilde{G}'$, if (V', E') is a subgraph of (V, E), a (vertex-)induced subgraph of (V, E), connected, or a connected component of (V, E), respectively.

4 Directed Graphs

In most of this Element we restrict our attention to undirected graphs – which we defined in Section 3.1 as graphs for which $(i, j) \in E$ if and only if $(j, i) \in E$ – as that is the setting in which most of the work has been done on the topics we cover. In this section we will take a brief detour to directed graphs – that is, graphs in which $(i, j) \in E$ and $(j, i) \notin E$ may both be true for given nodes $i, j \in V$ – and we give a brief overview of (a priori different) approaches to defining graph Laplacians on such graphs. Each of these approaches uses a different aspect of Laplacians on undirected graphs as a starting point to define a Laplacian on a directed graph.

For an edge-weighted directed graph, the edge weights ω need not be symmetric, that is, it is possible that $\omega_{ij} \neq \omega_{ji}$. We still assume $\omega_{ij} \geq 0$, with $\omega_{ij} > 0$ if and only if $(i, j) \in E$.

Figure 4.1 shows an example of a directed graph, where an arrow on an edge pointing from node i to node j indicates the edge (i, j). In particular, the graph in Figure 4.1 is an oriented graph, namely a directed graph in which $(i, j) \in E$ implies $(j, i) \notin E$. We do not require the directed graphs to be oriented.

A direct adaptation of the random walk graph Laplacian to directed graphs is given in Bauer [17]. In Zhou *et al.* [207] the authors make use of the one-to-one correspondence between directed graphs and bipartite graphs[29] to define new undirected graphs on the two independent vertex classes of the bipartite graph and combine the Laplacians on those new graphs into a Laplacian on the directed graph. In Chung [52] the author recalls the connection between graph Laplacians and random walks to define a graph Laplacian via a random walk on a directed graph. In Hein *et al.* [104] a similar approach is followed as

---

[28] In a slight abuse of notation $\chi_{E'}$ is viewed here as a function on $V' \times V'$ instead of E, such that $\chi_{E'}\omega_{V' \times V'}$ is the weight function that assigns ω_{ij} to $(i, j) \in V' \times V'$ if $(i, j) \in E'$ and that assigns 0 to $(i, j) \in V' \times V'$ otherwise.

[29] That is, graphs where the the vertex set can be partitioned into disjoint sets V_1 and V_2, the partite sets, such that every edge has exactly one endpoint in V_1 and one in V_2.

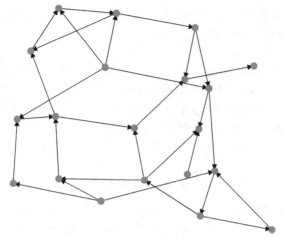

Figure 4.1 An example of a directed graph; specifically, an oriented graph.

we used[30] for our undirected Laplacian in Section 3, that is, the authors start by defining inner product structures on the spaces of node and edge functions and a discrete gradient, then find a divergence as the adjoint of the gradient and define the Laplacian as the divergence of the gradient. In Shubin [177] a *magnetic Laplacian* is introduced for physical reasons; in [86, 87, 100] it is used for community detection, visualization, and detection of hierarchical structures in directed graphs (see chapter 4 in [190]). In MacKay *et al.* [137] and Gong *et al.* [100] the *trophic Laplacian* is introduced, in Klus and Djurdjevac Conrad [119] the forward-backward Laplacian, and in Jost *et al.* [114] and Mulas *et al.* [158] the *non-backtracking Laplacian*. We refer to section 2.5 of [190] for more details on these approaches.

5 The Graph Ginzburg–Landau Functional

A central object in this work is the graph Ginzburg–Landau functional[31] $\mathrm{GL}_\varepsilon \colon \mathcal{V} \to \mathbb{R}$, which was first introduced in Bertozzi and Flenner [21, 22]. It consists of the Dirichlet energy plus a potential term:

$$\mathrm{GL}_\varepsilon(u) := \frac{1}{2}\alpha(\varepsilon)\|\nabla u\|_\varepsilon^2 + \frac{1}{\varepsilon}\mathcal{W}(u).$$

---

[30] More accurately, our Section 3 is mainly based on the setup in [189, 191] which in turn was based on [104].

[31] Not to be confused with the Ginzburg–Landau model for superconductivity. Other names for the (continuum version of the) functional may be encountered, especially in the continuum literature, such as Allen–Cahn, Cahn–Hilliard, Van der Waals–Cahn–Hilliard, or Modica–Mortola functional.

There are some variations in the literature regarding the choice of the ε-dependent factor $\alpha(\varepsilon)$ and the choice of potential term, which we briefly discuss here.

In [21, 22] the authors choose $\alpha(\varepsilon) = \varepsilon$ in analogy to the continuum Ginzburg–Landau functional (see section 3.7 in [190]). In Van Gennip and Bertozzi [189, section 3.1], however, the authors argue that, if one is interested in the limit $\varepsilon \downarrow 0$, then $\alpha(\varepsilon) = 1$ is a better choice. The reason for this is (in brief) that the divergence of the Dirichlet energy for which ε is meant to compensate in the continuum case, does not occur for the discrete graph Dirichlet energy, which remains bounded. Thus instead of compensating for divergent behaviour, a factor ε would completely remove the influence of the Dirichlet term in the limit $\varepsilon \downarrow 0$, leading to a trivial (and uninteresting) limit.

When considering the variational properties of GL_ε at a fixed $\varepsilon > 0$, the difference between $\alpha(\varepsilon) = \varepsilon$ and $\alpha(\varepsilon) = 1$ is minimal, since $\varepsilon^{-1/2} \, \mathrm{GL}_{\sqrt{\varepsilon}}$ with $\alpha(\varepsilon) = \varepsilon$ equals GL_ε with $\alpha = 1$. Moreover, if we consider gradient flows derived from GL_ε (see Section 7), going from $\alpha(\varepsilon) = \varepsilon$ to $\alpha(\varepsilon) = 1$ involves only a time rescaling $t_{\mathrm{new}} = t_{\mathrm{old}}/\varepsilon$.

The different choices in the potential term $\mathcal{W}$ concern two different issues. The first choice involves the factor d_i^r in the $\mathcal{V}$-inner product. In [21, 22] the authors use $\mathcal{W}(u) = \sum_{i \in V} W(u_i)$, where $W: \mathbb{R} \to \overline{\mathbb{R}} := \mathbb{R} \cup \{+\infty\}$ is a potential function, which we will consider in much more detail shortly. In Budd and Van Gennip [35] it is noted that $\mathcal{W}(u) = \langle W \circ u, 1 \rangle_{\mathcal{V}} = \sum_{i \in V} d_i^r W(u_i)$ is a preferable choice when studying the $\mathcal{V}$-gradient flow of GL_ε (see Section 7), as it removes the factor d_i^r (which, for $r \neq 0$, could be considered a node-dependent time rescaling) from the gradient flow.[32]

The second choice in $\mathcal{W}$ concerns the potential function $W: \mathbb{R} \to \overline{\mathbb{R}}$. In the classical continuum Ginzburg–Landau functional, this is a smooth double-well potential, whose graph resembles (a smooth variant of) the letter 'W'. An example is shown in Figure 5.1(a). Such a function has three important properties: smoothness, a global minimum which is achieved in exactly two locations (two 'wells'), and some kind of coercivity which implies that $W(x) \to \infty$ if $|x| \to \infty$. In some papers, such as in [189, section 2.3], no specific choice is made for W, but precise conditions are given for the smoothness, wells, and coercivity properties of W. Other papers choose a specific (quartic) potential from the class of potentials that satisfy these conditions, such as $W(x) = \frac{1}{4}(x^2 - 1)^2$ in [21, 22] or Van Gennip *et al.* [191, section 5] with wells at $x \in \{-1, 1\}$ or $W(x) = \frac{1}{4}x^2(x - 1)^2$ in Calatroni *et al.* [41] with wells at

---

[32] In fact, in [21, 22] this factor is also not present in the gradient flow, since in that paper a Euclidean inner product is used, that is, the $\mathcal{V}$-inner product with $r = 0$.

$x \in \{0, 1\}$. For most purposes, the location of the wells is not important.[33] A significant exception is the case of the signless Ginzburg–Landau functional, which we discuss in Section 5.3, and the graph Cahn–Hilliard equation (which requires a mass condition), which is addressed in Section 7.4.

When GL_ε is minimized, the potential term drives 'phase separation', that is, minimizers (especially at small $\varepsilon > 0$) will take values which are close to the values at which W has its wells (thus typically 0 and 1, or -1 and 1).

A significant departure from the standard double-well potential can be found in Budd *et al.* [35, 36, 37]. In those papers the double-obstacle potential is used (since it will be clear from the context which potential we are using at any given time in this Element, we use the same symbol W to denote it):

$$W(x) = \begin{cases} \frac{1}{2}x(1-x), & \text{if } 0 \le x \le 1, \\ +\infty, & \text{otherwise.} \end{cases} \tag{5.1}$$

Figure 5.1 (b) shows a visualization of the double-obstacle potential. We note that the double-obstacle potential also achieves its minimum in two wells, located at $x \in \{0, 1\}$, but the coercive nature of the potential is stronger than that of the double-well potential, with W attaining finite values only in the interval $[0, 1]$. We also call attention to the quadratic, rather than quartic, nature of the potential on $[0, 1]$. This is convenient when considering gradient flows in which the 'derivative' of W appears, which is linear on $(0, 1)$. A potential difficulty when using the double-obstacle potential compared to the double-well potential is that W is not differentiable outside of $(0, 1)$. We discuss these issues in

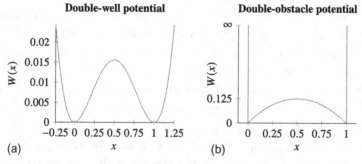

Figure 5.1 Two types of potential W that are commonly used in the Ginzburg–Landau functional: the double-well potential $W(x) = \frac{1}{4}x^2(x-1)^2$ (a) and the double-obstacle potential from (5.1) (b).

---

[33] The transformation $v = 2u - 1$ turns $u^2(u-1)^2$ into $\frac{1}{16}(v^2-1)^2$, and thus $\mathrm{GL}_\varepsilon(u)$ with potential $u^2(u-1)^2$ into $\frac{1}{4}\mathrm{GL}_\varepsilon(v)$ with potential $\frac{1}{4}(v^2-1)^2$.

more detail in Section 7 and in section 6 in [190], where we outline the results from [35, 36, 37].

5.1 Constraints

Minimizing GL_ε (in any of its variants that we have discussed) over $\mathcal{V}$ without imposing any further constraints, leads to constant minimizers $u = c$, where c can be the location of any of the wells of W.[34] Besides being necessary to avoid trivial minimizers, in applications constraints are often suggested naturally by a priori known information about the required solutions. In this Element we consider two common constraints:

- a 'hard' mass (or volume) constraint:[35] $\mathcal{M}(u) := \langle u, 1 \rangle_\mathcal{V} = M$, for a fixed and given $M \geq 0$;
- a 'soft' fidelity constraint, where a fidelity term of the form $\frac{1}{p} \|\mu^{\frac{1}{p}}(u-f)\|_{\mathcal{V},p}^p$ is added to to $GL_\varepsilon(u)$, where $\mu \in \mathcal{V}_{[0,\infty)} \setminus \{0\}$ is a node-dependent fidelity parameter function with support equal to some subset $Z \subseteq V$ and $f \in \mathcal{V}$ is a reference function to which fidelity should be 'softly' enforced on Z.

These constraints are discussed in more detail in [189, section 2.5] and play an important role in [35] (mass constraint) and [37] (fidelity constraint with $p = 2$).

The hard mass constraint can be directly included in the functional that has to be minimized by adding a term $\iota_{\{0\}}(\mathcal{M}(u) - M)$ to $GL_\varepsilon(u)$. In [13, 110] in related contexts relaxed mass constraints are used, in which upper and lower bounds are imposed for the mass instead of a precise value.

A graph functional consisting of the Dirichlet energy term and a fidelity term (or, in other words, a Ginzburg–Landau functional with fidelity term, but without potential term) is studied in Zhou and Schölkopf [205].

From an application-based point of view, the presence of a fidelity constraint usually differentiates graph classification from clustering (we refer to chapter 4 of [190] for more details).

5.2 Graph Cuts and Γ-Convergence to Total Variation

One important reason why minimization of GL_ε can be useful in applications that require clustering or classification of the node set of a graph, is that at small

---

[34] So $c \in \{-1, 1\}$ or $c \in \{0, 1\}$ for the specific double-well and double-obstacle potentials we have just discussed.
[35] Here, we use 'mass' and 'volume' interchangeably, as, if $S \subseteq V$, then $\mathcal{M}(\chi_S) = \text{vol}(S)$.

$\varepsilon > 0$ the functional GL_ε captures an (approximate) notion of perimeter of a node subset. To understand this, we first note that, for $S \subseteq V$,

$$TV(\chi_S) = \sum_{i \in S} \sum_{j \in S^c} \omega_{ij} =: Cut(S).$$

This quantity is called the graph cut of S and can be understood as a discrete perimeter (length) of S.

Since the graph cut is a measure for the strength of the connections between the sets S and S^c, it is a candidate for the objective function that is to be minimized in graph clustering. In practice it turns out that minimizing the graph cut subject only to the constraints that S and S^c are nonempty sets, often leads to an unbalanced clustering in which one of the two sets contains the vast majority of the graph nodes. In many applications this is not what is required, which has led to many 'balanced' (graph) cuts, such as the ratio cut [102], normalized cut [176], min-max cut [64], edge expansion (related to the sparsest cut problem) [10], and Cheeger cut[36] (or conductance) [49, 55]:

$$RCut(S) := \frac{Cut(S)}{|S|} + \frac{Cut(S)}{|S^c|}, \quad NCut(S) := \frac{Cut(S)}{vol(S)} + \frac{Cut(S)}{vol(S^c)},$$

$$MCut(S) := \frac{Cut(S)}{\sum_{\substack{i \in S \\ j \in S}} \omega_{ij}} + \frac{Cut(S)}{\sum_{\substack{i \in S^c \\ j \in S^c}} \omega_{ij}}, \quad ECut(S) := \frac{Cut(S)}{\min(|S|, |S^c|)},$$

$$\text{and} \quad CCut(S) := \frac{Cut(S)}{\min(vol(S), vol(S^c))},$$

respectively, where $r = 1$ is used in the computations of the volume. Since the main interest in these cuts is as objective functions in minimization problems, different versions of the cuts that are equivalent for minimization purposes may be encountered, such as $\frac{Cut(S)}{|S||S^c|}$ for the ratio cut, which differs from the preceding definition above only by a constant factor $\frac{1}{|V|}$.

These balanced cuts have been normalized by factors which, upon minimization, avoid one of the sets S and S^c being much larger than the other, where 'large' is to be interpreted according to the specific measure used in the normalizing factors. Intuitively, these normalization factors play a role similar to the mass constraint from Section 5.1. Minimization of such balanced cuts is NP-hard (see, for example, [176, 193] and references therein). For more information about relaxations of some of these minimization problems in terms of eigenvalue problems for graph Laplacians, we refer to von Luxburg [193].

---

[36] The minimal value $\min_{S \subseteq V} CCut(S)$ is called the Cheeger constant (see also (6.1)). Some sources, such as [55, section 2.3], also speak of the edge expansion in this context.

Multiclass extensions of the preceding cuts for a partition $\{S_i\}_{i \in I}$ of V are straightforward to construct: $\sum_{i \in I} \frac{\text{Cut}(S_i)}{|S_i|}$ for the ratio cut, $\sum_{i \in I} \frac{\text{cut}S_i}{\min(|S_i|, |S_i^c|)}$ for the edge expansion, and similarly for the other balanced cuts.

For more details about graph cuts, we refer to Izenman [109, chapter 11].

The following theorem shows the connection between the graph cut and GL_ε. It uses the language of Γ-convergence [28, 62].

Theorem 5.1. *Assume that W is either a smooth double-well potential with wells[37] at $x \in \{0, 1\}$, satisfying the coercivity condition $\lim_{|x| \to \infty} W(x) = \infty$, or is the double-obstacle potential. Let $\mathcal{W}$ be defined in either of the two ways that are introduced near the beginning of (the current) Section 5 and let $\alpha(\varepsilon) = 1$.*
When $\varepsilon \downarrow 0$, the sequence (GL_ε) Γ-converges to the functional:

$$\text{GL}_0 : \mathcal{V} \to \overline{\mathbb{R}}, \qquad \text{GL}_0 : u \mapsto \begin{cases} \text{TV}(u), & \text{if } u \in \mathcal{V}_{\{0,1\}}, \\ +\infty, & \text{otherwise.} \end{cases}$$

Moreover, the following compactness result holds: if (ε_k) is a sequence of strictly positive real numbers converging to zero and (u_k) is a sequence in $\mathcal{V}$ for which $\text{GL}_{\varepsilon_k}(u_k)$ is bounded uniformly in k, then there exists a subsequence of (u_k) which converges to a $u_\infty \in \mathcal{V}$.

Proof. In the double-well case, the proof can be found in [189, theorems 3.1 and 3.2]. In the double-obstacle case, the proof of Γ-convergence is very similar and given in [35, theorem 6.1]. The proof of the compactness result is not given there, but it is simpler than the one in [189, theorem 3.2]: the double-obstacle potential forces the functions u_k to lie in the compact set $\mathcal{V}_{[0,1]}$. Compactness of $\mathcal{V}_{[0,1]}$ is a consequence of the Heine–Borel theorem, if we identify the set with the closed and bounded set of vectors $[0, 1]^n \subseteq \mathbb{R}^n$.

The proof in [189] works with $\mathcal{W}(u) = \sum_{i \in V} W(u_i)$, while the proof in [35] has $\mathcal{W}(u) = \langle W \circ u, 1 \rangle_{\mathcal{V}}$. □

As a consequence of Theorem 5.1, by the fundamental theorem of Γ-convergence (see [28, 62]), if (u_k) is a sequence such that u_k minimizes $\text{GL}_{\varepsilon_k}$ over $\mathcal{V}$, then any cluster point of the sequence minimizes GL_0. Of course, that in itself is not very interesting, as we already know that the minimizers of GL_ε over $\mathcal{V}$ are constant functions. In [189, theorem 3.6] it is shown that the results of Theorem 5.1 remain true (mutatis mutandis) if any one of the constraints from Section 5.1 is implemented in the double-well case and [33, theorem 7.2.4,

---

[37] The specific placement of the wells is not crucial, but the domain on which GL_0 is finite, as well as the multiplicative factor in $\text{GL}_0(u)$ (currently '1') needed to turn $|u_i - u_j|$ into $(u_i - u_j)^2$ at the values in the wells, would have to be adapted to reflect any alternative choice.

corollary 7.2.5] shows the same for the double-obstacle case with a fidelity constraint. The double-obstacle case with a mass constraint can be tackled with similar techniques as the other cases.

5.3 Signless Laplacians and Signless Ginzburg–Landau Functional

A variant of the graph Ginzburg–Landau functional is the *signless* graph Ginzburg–Landau functional $GL_\varepsilon^\sigma : V \to \mathbb{R}$:

$$GL_\varepsilon^\sigma(u) := \frac{1}{2}\alpha(\varepsilon)\|\nabla^\sigma u\|_{\mathcal{E}}^2 + \frac{1}{\varepsilon}W(u),$$

where the signless graph gradient is defined to be $(\nabla^\sigma u)_{ij} := \omega_{ij}^{1-q}(u_j + u_i)$. We note that the only difference with the standard graph gradient and graph Ginzburg–Landau functional is the sum rather than the difference of u_j and u_i in the gradient. In Keetch and Van Gennip [117] and Keetch [116], minimization of GL_ε^σ is used to find approximate solutions to the Max-Cut problem, which consists of finding a partition of the node set V into $S \subseteq V$ and S^c, in such a way that Cut (S) is maximized. As before near the beginning of Section 5, we note that the choice between $\alpha(\varepsilon) = 1$ and $\alpha(\varepsilon) = \varepsilon$ is not relevant for this minimization problem. The choice of W, however, is important. In particular, the wells of W should be placed symmetrically with respect to the origin, otherwise the constant function $u = 0$ would be the unique minimizer. In [116, 117] the authors use $W(x) = (x^2 - 1)^2$, $W(u) = \sum_{i \in V} W(u_i)$, $\alpha(\varepsilon) = 1$, and $q = 1$. We note that no additional constraints, such as a mass or fidelity constraint, are required to avoid trivial minimizers of GL_ε^σ.

.   As for the standard graph gradient, we can define the signless graph divergence as the adjoint of the signless gradient. Having those ingredients, we then define the signless graph Laplacian as the signless divergence of the signless gradient, the signless graph Dirichlet energy as in (3.8), but using the signless gradient instead, and signless graph total variation as in (3.10), but using the signless divergence instead. In each of these cases, this simply translates to replacing the difference in the divergence or Laplacian by a summation. In particular,

$$(\Delta^\sigma u)_i := d_i^{-r} \sum_{j \in V} \omega_{ij}(u_i + u_j) \quad \text{and} \quad TV^\sigma(u) := \frac{1}{2}\sum_{i,j \in V} \omega_{ij}|u_i + u_j|. \quad (5.2)$$

We note that the signless Laplacian has matrix representation $\Delta^\sigma = D^{-r}(D+A)$ (see Remark 3.4). Besides the combinatorial ($r=0$) and random walk ($r=1$) versions, the symmetrically normalized signless Laplacian $\Delta^{\sigma,\text{sym}} = D^{-\frac{1}{2}}(D + A)D^{-\frac{1}{2}}$ also appears in the literature. It is a special case of the signless variant of the two-parameter graph Laplacian in (3.7) (see also Remark 3.6).

The signless analogue of Theorem 5.1 holds, with GL_ε, TV, and $\mathcal{V}_{\{0,1\}}$ replaced by GL_ε^σ, TV^σ, and $\mathcal{V}_{\{-1,1\}}$, respectively, as proven in [117, lemmas 4.3 and 4.4]. This justifies the use of GL_ε^+ as an approximate objective function for the Max-Cut problem, since, for $S \subseteq V$, $TV^\sigma(\chi_S - \chi_{S^c}) = 2\sum_{i,j \in V} \omega_{ij} - 4\text{Cut}(S)$ [117, lemma 4.1]. Thus minimization of $TV^\sigma(\chi_S - \chi_{S^c})$ over S maximizes the cut. We note that, given that the wells of W are located at $x \in \{-1, 1\}$, the relevant set 'indicator' function is here $\chi_S - \chi_{S^c}$, not χ_S.

6 Spectrum of the Graph Laplacians

Indicators of the usefulness of the graph Laplacians for clustering problems can be found in their spectrum, particularly the property that is stated in the following lemma. In this section (Section 6), we temporarily drop the assumption that our graphs are connected. We begin with a very important result.

Lemma 6.1. *All eigenvalues of Δ and Δ^{sym} are real and nonnegative. The smallest eigenvalue of each of these operators is 0 and its algebraic and geometric multiplicities are both equal to the number $k \in \mathbb{N}$ of connected components $G_1, \ldots, G_k$ of the graph G. The associated eigenspace for Δ is spanned by the set of indicator functions (on V) $\{\chi_{S^i}\}_{i \in [k]}$, where $S^i \subseteq V$ is the set of nodes that induces the subgraph G_i. The associated eigenspace for Δ^{sym} is spanned by $\{f^i\}_{i \in [k]}$ where $f^i: V \to \mathbb{R}$ is defined by, for all $j \in V$, $f_j^i := d_j^{1/2}(\chi_{S^i})_j$.*

Proof. This well-known result has been proven and reproven in many places, for example Chung [55, lemma 1.7] and von Luxburg [193, propositions 1–4]. □

This lemma shows that if the clustering problem is trivial, in the sense that each cluster is its own connected component, then the number of clusters is given by the multiplicity of the zero eigenvalue and the corresponding eigenspace contains information about the nodes belonging to each cluster. The expectation that graph Laplacians are also useful in nontrivial clustering problems, in which the graph itself may be connected, but certain induced subgraphs have a high edge volume (see (3.2)) and low connectivity to other parts of the graph, is based on the hope that small perturbations to the edge structure of the trivial case will preserve the important information in the first (in ascending order) eigenvalues of the graph Laplacian and their corresponding eigenfunctions (or eigenspaces). This hope is (non-rigorously) justified in practice by the success of Laplacian-based clustering techniques, such as spectral clustering [109, 161, 176, 193] or the ones discussed in [190].

This hope can also be given some rigorous support, for example through higher-order Cheeger inequalities (see Lee *et al.* [128, theorem 1.1])[38] of the form (for $K \in \mathbb{N} \cap [2,n]$),

$$\frac{1}{2}\lambda_K \leq \min_{\{S_k\}_{k=1}^K} \max \left\{ \frac{\text{Cut}(S_k)}{\text{vol}(S_k)} : k \in [K] \right\} \leq C(K)\sqrt{\lambda_K}, \qquad (6.1)$$

where λ_K denotes the Kth eigenvalue (in nondecreasing order) of the random walk graph Laplacian and $C(K) = \mathcal{O}(K^2)$ as $K \to \infty$.[39] The minimum in (6.1) is taken over all partitions of V into K (per definition of partition nonempty and pairwise disjoint) subsets S_k of V. These inequalities tell us that, if there is a large gap between the Kth and $(K+1)^{\text{st}}$ eigenvalues, then the value of the Cheeger constant, that is, the value in between the inequalities in (6.1) (see also footnote 36), will be significantly higher if we partition V into $K+1$ subsets, than if we partition it into K subsets.

For further details about the eigenvectors that support their use in clustering, we refer to the structure theorems of Peng *et al.* [169] and Macgregor and Sun [136] (see also Macgregor [133, chapter 4]). In Macgregor and Sun [136] (see also Macgregor [133, chapter 5]) it is shown that in some cases the use of fewer than K eigenvectors (specifically, in the spectral clustering method; see section 4.1.2 in [190]) to find K clusters can be beneficial.

More rigorous support is given by the results of Hoffmann *et al.* [105], whose paper looked at graph Laplacians $\Delta^{(s,t)}$ (see (3.7)) that are built upon data sampled from a probability density which is a perturbation of perfectly separated clusters, and the continuum limit of these Laplacians obtained as the number of data points tends to infinity (more details on this continuum object and this random setting can be found in section 7.2 in [190]). It was shown in [105, theorem 3.2] that if $s + t = 1$ (as is the case for the random walk and symmetrically normalized Laplacians), then this continuum operator has a spectral gap between its second and third eigenvalue which is independent of the size of the perturbation (refer to [190] for more details).

The second smallest eigenvalue of a graph Laplacian[40] is called the *algebraic connectivity* or *Fiedler value*. By Lemma 6.1, for a connected graph this

---

[38] These inequalities are generalizations of the Cheeger (constant) inequality for $K = 2$; see for example Alon and Milman [8], Alon [7], Sinclair and Jerrum [178], or Chung [55, chapter 2]. We note that if $K = 2$, then the maximum in (6.1) is the Cheeger cut CCut from Section 5.2.

[39] This means that there exist constants $C_1, C_2 > 0$ such that for all $K \geq C_1$, $|C(K)| \leq C_2 K^2$.

[40] Commonly the combinatorial graph Laplacian is used to define the Fiedler value and Fiedler vector, yet in practical (clustering) applications other Laplacians are used as well, often with greater success. See, for example, Bertozzi and Flenner [21, 22, section 2.4]). In Le Gorrec *et al.* [127] it is argued that the eigenvector corresponding to the second-largest eigenvalue of the adjacency matrix, where the latter is first scaled (for example, by way of Knight and Ruiz [120]) into the double-stochastic form $D_1 A D_2$ (i.e., each row and each column of $D_1 A D_2$ sums to one) with D_1 and D_2 diagonal matrices, has a structure that more clearly indicates cluster structure than Fiedler vectors.

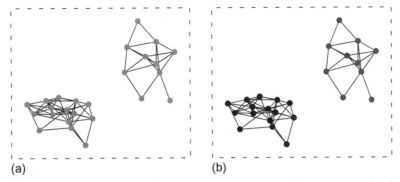

Figure 6.1 An example of a disconnected graph (a) and that same graph with nodes coloured according to the value of the Fiedler vector at that node (b).

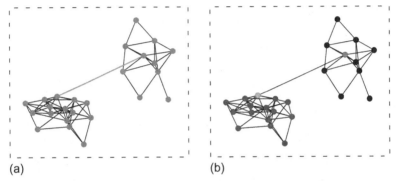

Figure 6.2 The graph from Figure 6.1 with an extra edge added to make it connected (a) and that same connected graph with nodes coloured according to the value of the Fiedler vector at that node (b).

value is strictly positive. The associated eigenvector is called the *Fiedler vector*.[41]

We illustrate these properties in Figures 6.1, 6.2, and 6.3. Figure 6.1 shows a disconnected graph, and Figure 6.1 (b) shows how the Fiedler vector distinguishes between the connected components of the graph. Figure 6.3 (a) shows the spectrum of the associated unnormalized graph Laplacian, and we observe that the first two eigenvalues are zero, in accordance with Lemma 6.1. Next, in Figure 6.2 we make this graph connected by adding a single extra edge. Figure 6.2 (b) shows how the Fiedler vector still distinguishes between the two clusters. Figure 6.3 (b) shows the spectrum of the associated graph Laplacian, and we observe that the second eigenvalue is now non-zero – in accordance with Lemma 6.1 – but the other eigenvalues are largely unchanged.

---

[41] The associated eigenspace can have dimension two or higher, yet the literature typically speaks about *the* Fiedler vector.

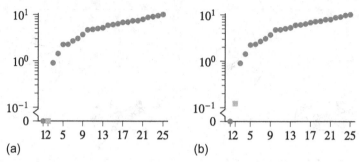

Figure 6.3 The spectra of the (unnormalized) graph Laplacians of the graphs from Figure 6.1 (a) and Figure 6.2 (b), plotted on a (crunched) log scale to emphasize the change in the second eigenvalue, indicated by a square marker.

One key feature of the Laplacian spectrum is its stability with respect to noise. In El Karoui and Wu [115, lemmas 3.1 and 3.2] it was shown that if there exist $(\alpha_i)_{i=1}^n$ and $\varepsilon > 0$ such that for all $i, j \in V$, $\alpha_i > 0$ and $|\omega_{i,j} - \alpha_i \tilde{\omega}_{i,j}| \leq \varepsilon$,[42] then the corresponding random walk Laplacians built from ω and $\tilde{\omega}$ differ in spectral norm[43] by at most an $\mathcal{O}(\varepsilon)$ term which is independent of the α_i. For a more comprehensive discussion of this stability, we refer to Ding and Wu [65] and the references therein. This property is of practical importance, as it allows (spectral) graph Laplacian methods to be applied robustly to noisy data.

There are other properties of the spectrum that can be proven rigorously. Since we will not directly use them in the current work, we refer to other sources such as [55, 191, 193] for more information.

An analogous result to Lemma 6.1 also holds for the signless graph Laplacians (see Section 5.3). We recall the definition of bipartite graphs from footnote 29.

Lemma 6.2. *All eigenvalues of Δ^σ and $\Delta^{\sigma,sym}$ are real and nonnegative. Assume the graph G has $k \in \mathbb{N}$ connected components $G_1, \ldots, G_k$ induced by the subsets $S^i \subseteq V$ ($i \in [k]$) and let $k' \in \mathbb{N} \cap [0, k]$. Then both Δ^σ and $\Delta^{\sigma,sym}$ have eigenvalue 0 with algebraic and geometric multiplicity each equal to k' if and only if k' of the connected components are bipartite graphs.*

In that case we may assume (possibly after relabelling) that, for all $i \in [k']$, G_i is bipartite. Denote the partite sets of G_i by $T^i \subseteq S^i$ and $S^i \setminus T^i$. Then the eigenspace corresponding to the eigenvalue 0 for Δ^σ is spanned by the set of

---

[42] And $\min_{i \in V} \frac{1}{n} \sum_{j \in V, j \neq i} \omega_{ij} > \varepsilon$. We note that here we have taken $G = \tilde{G} = 1$ in [115, lemmas 2.1, 2.2, and 2.3] to align their setting with ours.

[43] The spectral norm of a matrix is its largest singular value, namely the square root of the largest eigenvalue of the product of the transpose (or conjugate transpose for complex matrices) of the matrix and the matrix itself (in either order).

indicator functions (on V) $\{\chi_{T^i} - \chi_{S^i\backslash T^i}\}_{i \in [k^i]}$. *The eigenspace corresponding to the eigenvalue 0 for $\Delta^{\sigma, sym}$ is spanned by $\{f^i\}_{i \in [k^i]}$ where the functions f^i : $V \to \mathbb{R}$ are defined by, for all $j \in V$, $f^i_j := d^{1/2}_j \left[(\chi_{T^i})_j - (\chi_{S^i\backslash T^i})_j \right]$.*

Proof. A proof is provided in Keetch and Van Gennip [117, proposition 4]. $\square$

Similar to how the result from Lemma 6.1 helps interpreting the usefulness of graph Laplacians for clustering, so the result from Lemma 6.2 clarifies the usefulness of signless graph Laplacians for Max-Cut problems, as in [116, 117]. The objective in a Max-Cut problem is to find a partition of the node set V of a given graph into two disjoint nonempty subsets T and $V \setminus T$ such that Cut $(T) = \max_{\tilde{T} \subseteq V}$ Cut $(\tilde{T})$ (see Section 5.2). In the trivial case, that is, for a graph in which all k connected components are bipartite) the maximum cut can be achieved by setting $T = \bigcup_{i=1}^k T_i$ (using the notation from Lemma 6.2) and the information about each T_i is encoded in the eigenspace corresponding to the eigenvalue 0. Analogously to the clustering case, the hope (justified by numerical tests in [116, 117]) is that, if the connected components are perturbations of bipartite graphs, enough of this information remains encoded in those eigenfunctions (or eigenspaces) that correspond to the smallest eigenvalues of the signless graph Laplacians, such that it can be used to construct a partition of V that, in a sense,[44] is the closest to an actual bipartition as is possible in the given graph (or a good approximation thereof).

For information about the (nonlinear) spectrum of graph p-Laplacians, we refer to Bühler and Hein [38].

7 Gradient Flow: Allen–Cahn

Starting from this section, we only consider undirected graphs. In the definition of GL_ε, we make the choices $\alpha(\varepsilon) = 1$ and $\mathcal{W}(u) = \langle W \circ u, 1 \rangle_\mathcal{V}$.[45] We will specify whether W is a double-well or double-obstacle potential where this is relevant. Also, we recall from Remark 3.9 that we choose $q = 1$.

In Section 5 we have argued that minimizing GL_ε under a mass or fidelity constraint gives constrained approximate minimum cuts. This raises the question of how a minimizer can be found. We introduce three different options aimed at minimizing (or approximately minimizing) GL_ε: a gradient flow (in the current section), a threshold dynamics scheme (Section 8), and flow by

---

[44] Namely in the sense that it leads to (a good approximation of) the maximum cut value for that graph.

[45] Some of the sources that are cited throughout may make different choices. Unless these choices strongly impact the claims and results we present here, we will not draw attention to such differences.

mean curvature (Section 9). It should be noted that none of these options prov-
ably leads to global minimizers of GL_ε, but in many cases it can be shown that
the scheme in question decreases GL_ε (or a closely related functional).

This work focuses on graph models, not the continuum models that were their
inspiration, and so we will not delve deeply into those models. In section 3.7 of
[190] we give a short (and very much not exhaustive) overview of some of the
important literature on the continuum models that inspired many of the graph
models we discuss in this work.

7.1 Smooth Double-Well Potential

First we consider the $\mathcal{V}$-gradient flow of GL_ε [21, 22, 191]. The equation
describing this flow is of the form $\frac{du}{dt} = -\operatorname{grad}_\mathcal{V} \mathrm{GL}_\varepsilon(u)$, where for all $u \in \mathcal{V}$,
the $\mathcal{V}$-gradient of GL_ε at u is the unique function $\operatorname{grad}_\mathcal{V} \mathrm{GL}_\varepsilon(u) \in \mathcal{V}$ such that,
with $s \in \mathbb{R}$ and for all $v \in \mathcal{V}$,

$$\frac{d}{ds} \mathrm{GL}_\varepsilon(u + sv)\bigg|_{s=0} = \langle \operatorname{grad}_\mathcal{V} \mathrm{GL}_\varepsilon(u), v \rangle_\mathcal{V}.$$

In analogy to the continuum case (see section 3.7.2 of [190]), the resulting
equation is called the graph Allen–Cahn equation:

$$\frac{du}{dt} = -\Delta u - \frac{1}{\varepsilon} W' \circ u. \tag{7.1}$$

We have assumed here that the double-well potential W is chosen to be smooth
(in the sense of Section 5) and, as is standard practice for gradient flows, we
have introduced an 'artificial time' variable t, such that at each time t, $u(t) \in \mathcal{V}$.
To be precise, borrowing notation from Budd and Van Gennip [35], we define
the following spaces, given an interval $T \subseteq \mathbb{R}$ and subset $A \subseteq \mathbb{R}$:

$$\mathcal{V}_{t \in T} := \{u \colon T \to \mathcal{V}\}, \qquad \mathcal{V}_{A, t \in T} := \{u \colon T \to \mathcal{V}_A\},$$
$$L^2(T; \mathcal{V}) := \{u \in \mathcal{V}_{t \in T} \colon \|u\|_{t \in T} < \infty\},$$
$$H^1(T; \mathcal{V}) := \{u \in L^2(T; \mathcal{V}) \colon \frac{du}{dt} \in L^2(T; \mathcal{V})\},$$
$$H^1_{\mathrm{loc}}(T; \mathcal{V}) := \{u \in \mathcal{V}_{t \in T} \colon \forall a, b \in T \; u|_{(a,b)} \in H^1((a,b); \mathcal{V})\}.$$

The norm $\| \cdot \|_{t \in T}$ in the definition of $L^2(T; \mathcal{V})$ is induced by the inner product

$$(u, v)_{t \in T} := \int_T \langle u(t), v(t) \rangle_\mathcal{V} \, dt$$

and $\frac{du}{dt} \in L^2(T; \mathcal{V})$ denotes the generalized time derivative of u, that is, the
function which satisfies, for all $v \in C_c^\infty(T; \mathcal{V})$, $\left(u, \frac{dv}{dt}\right)_{t \in T} = -\left(\frac{du}{dt}, v\right)_{t \in T}$.

Remark 7.1. If we were not to choose $\alpha(\varepsilon) = 1$, but leave $\alpha(\varepsilon)$ unspecified, then (7.1) would be

$$\frac{du}{dt} = -\alpha(\varepsilon)\Delta u - \frac{1}{\varepsilon}W' \circ u$$

instead. Rescaling by $\alpha(\varepsilon)$ gives

$$\frac{1}{\alpha(\varepsilon)}\frac{du}{dt} = -\Delta u - \frac{1}{\varepsilon\alpha(\varepsilon)}W' \circ u \quad \text{or} \quad \frac{du}{dt} = -\Delta u - \frac{1}{\tilde{\varepsilon}}W' \circ u,$$

if we define $\tilde{t} = \alpha(\varepsilon)^{-1}t$ and $\tilde{\varepsilon} = \varepsilon\alpha(\varepsilon)$. So, even though the choice of $\alpha(\varepsilon)$ matters when considering the limiting behaviour of GL_ε as $\varepsilon \downarrow 0$ (see Theorem 5.1), when considering the graph Allen–Cahn equation we can assume, without loss of generality, that $\alpha(\varepsilon) = 1$, as indeed we did earlier in this section and as will be our default choice except where it is relevant to specify otherwise.

The choice of $\mathcal{W}$ has more influence on the Allen–Cahn equation. Choosing $\mathcal{W}(u) = \sum_{i\in V} W(u_i)$ (rather than $\mathcal{W}(u) = \langle W\circ u, 1\rangle_V$) leads to a term $-\frac{1}{\varepsilon}D^{-r}W' \circ u$ (if we interpret $W' \circ u$ as the vector with components $W'(u_i)$ for $i \in V$) instead of $-\frac{1}{\varepsilon}W' \circ u$. To the authors' knowledge, there are currently no studies that focus on the influence that the extra scaling D^{-r} (if $r \neq 0$) has in practical applications. In our discussion of applications in chapter 4 of [190], we will mostly ignore this difference.

Remark 7.2. If we wish to similarly obtain a graph Allen–Cahn equation with the two-parameter normalization of the graph Laplacian $\Delta^{(s_1,s_2)}$ (which, we recall from (3.7), is defined to be $D^{-s_1}(D - A)D^{-s_2}$), that is,

$$\frac{du}{dt} = -\Delta^{(s_1,s_2)}u - \frac{1}{\varepsilon}W' \circ u,$$

as a V-gradient flow of a Ginzburg–Landau-like energy, then we must modify the Ginzburg–Landau energy to

$$\frac{1}{2}\|\nabla(D^{-s_2}u)\|_{\tilde{\varepsilon}}^2 + \frac{1}{\varepsilon}\mathcal{W}(u),$$

and take the V-gradient flow (and inner products in the energy) with $r=s_1-s_2$. The same modification mutatis mutandis applies to all of the Allen–Cahn equations in (this) Section 7. For further details, we refer to Budd [34].

Remark 7.3. Since the right-hand side of (7.1) is locally Lipschitz continuous, by the Picard–Lindelöf theorem (see Hale [103, chapter I, theorem 3.1]), for every $u^0 \in V$ there exists a unique continuously differentiable solution u locally in time of the initial-value problem with Equation (7.1) and initial condition $u(0) = u_0$. Since (7.1) is the V-gradient flow of GL_ε, we have, for all

$t \geq 0$ in the domain of u, $\mathrm{GL}_\varepsilon(u(t)) \leq \mathrm{GL}_\varepsilon(u_0) < \infty$. Since W satisfies a coercivity condition (i.e., $W(x) \to \infty$ if $|x| \to \infty$; see Section 5), this implies that $\|u(t)\|_{\mathcal{V},\infty}$ is bounded for all $t \geq 0$ in the domain of u (there is no finite-time blowup). A standard continuation result for ODEs [103, chapter I, theorem 2.1] tells us that the solution u exists for all $t \in [0, \infty)$.

Remark 7.4. As discussed in some more detail in section 3.7.6 of [190], solutions of the continuum Allen–Cahn equation converge to solutions of continuum mean curvature flow (in some sense that can be made precise) as $\varepsilon \downarrow 0$. For more details about the expectations this raises for the graph variants, we refer to Section 9.2.

Remark 7.5. In Keetch and Van Gennip [117] (see also Keetch [116]) the signless graph Allen–Cahn equation is derived, based on the signless graph Ginzburg–Landau functional from Section 5.3. It differs from the equation in (7.1) in that it uses the signless graph Laplacian Δ^σ from (5.2) rather than Δ.

7.2 Double-Obstacle Potential

Instead of using a smooth double-well potential W, we can also consider the $\mathcal{V}$-gradient flow of GL_ε using the nondifferentiable double-obstacle potential. In that case $\mathrm{grad}_\mathcal{V}\, \mathrm{GL}_\varepsilon(u)$ is no longer uniquely determined at each u. Instead we require the use of subgradients [67, definition 5.1] and the differential equation describing the gradient flow is replaced by a differential inclusion, $\frac{du}{dt} \in -\partial_\mathcal{V}\, \mathrm{GL}_\varepsilon(u)$, where the subdifferential $\partial_\mathcal{V}\, \mathrm{GL}_\varepsilon(u)$ of GL_ε at $u \in \mathcal{V}$ (with respect to the $\mathcal{V}$-inner product) is the set[46]

$$\begin{cases} \{\beta \in \mathcal{V}: \forall w \in \mathcal{V} \;\; \langle w - u, \beta \rangle_\mathcal{V} + \mathrm{GL}_\varepsilon(u) \leq \mathrm{GL}_\varepsilon(w)\}, & \text{if } \mathrm{GL}_\varepsilon(u) < +\infty, \\ \emptyset, & \text{if } \mathrm{GL}_\varepsilon(u) = +\infty. \end{cases}$$

Using the double-obstacle potential in GL_ε then gives us the following gradient flow differential inclusion:[47]

---

[46] Per the general definition of the subdifferential in Ekeland and Temam [67, definition 5.1], β should be in the topological dual of $\mathcal{V}$. Since $\mathcal{V}$ is a finite-dimensional inner product space (and thus also a Hilbert space), it is reflexive and we identify $\mathcal{V}$ with its topological dual.

[47] The (negative) subdifferential is given by

$$-\partial_\mathbb{R}\, \iota_{[0,1]}(u_i(t)) = \begin{cases} [0, \infty), & \text{if } u_i(t) = 0, \\ \{0\}, & \text{if } 0 < u_i(t) < 1, \\ (-\infty, 0], & \text{if } u_i(t) = 1, \\ \emptyset, & \text{if } u_i(t) < 0 \text{ or } u_i(t) > 1. \end{cases}$$

$$\frac{du}{dt} = -\Delta u + \frac{1}{\varepsilon}\left(-\frac{1}{2} + u + \beta\right), \text{ where, } \forall i \in V, \beta_i(t) \in -\partial_{\mathbb{R}}\iota_{[0,1]}(u_i(t)). \quad (7.2)$$

We define a solution of (7.2) on an interval $T \subseteq \mathbb{R}$ to be a pair $(u, \beta) \in \mathcal{V}_{[0,1],t\in T} \times \mathcal{V}_{t\in T}$ with $u \in H^1_{\mathrm{loc}}(T; V) \cap C^0(T; V)$ such that (7.2) is satisfied at a.e. $t \in T$ and for all $i \in V$.[48] In Budd and Van Gennip [35, theorem 3.2] it is proven that if (u, β) is a solution to (7.2), then β is determined at all $i \in V$ and a.e. $t \in T$ to be

$$\beta_i(t) = \begin{cases} \frac{1}{2} + \varepsilon(\Delta u(t))_i, & \text{if } u_i(t) = 0, \\ 0, & \text{if } u_i(t) \in (0, 1), \\ -\frac{1}{2} + \varepsilon(\Delta u(t))_i, & \text{if } u_i(t) = 1. \end{cases}$$

This means that the differential inclusion above is actually a differential equation.

When discussing the Allen–Cahn equation with the double-obstacle potential from (7.2), we have stated the result for a.e. $t \in T$. This contrasts with the Allen–Cahn equation with the double-well potential from (7.1), for which we have seen in Remark 7.3 that, for every initial condition, a unique solution exists on $[0, \infty)$. In [35, theorems 3.9 and 3.10] it is shown that, for all initial conditions $u^0 \in \mathcal{V}_{[0,1]}$ there exists a pair $(u, \beta) \in \mathcal{V}_{[0,1],t\in T} \times \mathcal{V}_{t\in T}$ which satisfies (7.2) for a.e. $t \in T$ with $u(0) = u^0$ and $u \in H^1_{\mathrm{loc}}(T; V) \cap C^{0,1}(T; V)$. Moreover, u is uniquely determined for *all* $t \in T$ and β for a.e. $t \in T$.

The choice for the double-obstacle potential makes it possible to connect the graph Allen–Cahn equation with the graph Merriman–Bence–Osher (MBO) scheme, which we introduce in Section 8. This connection is looked at in more detail in chapter 6 of [190].

Also, (numerical) practice is influenced by the choice for the double-obstacle potential, as argued in Bosch *et al.* [26], where the (fidelity-forced; see Section 7.3) graph Allen–Cahn equation with a non-smooth potential outperforms the one with a smooth potential on image segmentation tasks (for more detail on image segmentation, we refer to section 4.1.3 of [190]).

7.3 Allen–Cahn with Constraints

We can incorporate the mass constraint or fidelity constraint from Section 5.1 into the gradient flow. Starting with the latter, recall that the fidelity term $\frac{1}{p}\|\mu^{1/p}(u - f)\|^p_{\mathcal{V},p}$ is added to $\mathrm{GL}_\varepsilon(u)$, where $\mu \in \mathcal{V}_{[0,\infty)} \setminus \{0\}$ has support $Z \subseteq V$. For simplicity we restrict ourselves here to the case $p = 2$. This is also most commonly used in the literature, for example, Bertozzi and Flenner

---

[48] We may sometimes simply refer to u as a solution, implying the existence of a corresponding β.

[21, 22] (double-well potential) and Budd *et al.* [37] (double-obstacle potential). At the level of the $\mathcal{V}$-gradient flow equation, this adds a term $-\mu(u - f)$ (i.e., minus the first variation of the fidelity term in the functional) to the right-hand side of (7.1) or (7.2), leading to the fidelity-forced Allen–Cahn equation on graphs:

$$\frac{du}{dt} = -\Delta u - \frac{1}{\varepsilon} g(u, \beta) - \mu(u - f), \qquad (7.3)$$

where $g(u, \beta) = W' \circ u$ for the double-well potential case (see (7.1)) and $g(u, \beta) = \frac{1}{2} - u - \beta$ for the double-obstacle potential case (see (7.2)).

To instead impose a mass constraint $\mathcal{M}(u) = M$, we recall from Section 5.1 that we can do so by adding the term $\iota_{\{0\}}(\mathcal{M}(u) - M)$ to the functional. In the gradient flow this leads to an additional term [67, proposition 5.6] which should be an element of the subdifferential $\partial_{\mathcal{V}} m(u)$, where $m(u) := \iota_{\{0\}}(\mathcal{M}(u) - M)$.

Lemma 7.6. *Let $u \in V$ and $M \in \mathbb{R}$, then*

$$\partial_{\mathcal{V}} m(u) = \begin{cases} \{v \in \mathcal{V} : \exists c \in \mathbb{R} \ \forall i \in V \ v_i = c\}, & \text{if } \mathcal{M}(u) = M, \\ \emptyset, & \text{if } \mathcal{M}(u) \neq M. \end{cases}$$

Proof. The proof is found in lemma 3.1.6 in [190]. □

Lemma 7.6 shows that, if a mass constraint is imposed, an additional constant term is added to the gradient flow. The value of this constant is determined by the requirement that the resulting equation conserves mass. To be explicit, if $\frac{du}{dt} = -\Delta u - \frac{1}{\varepsilon} g(u, \beta) + c$ (recall the definition of $g(u, \beta)$ from its introduction in the fidelity-forced case), then we require

$$0 = \frac{d}{dt}\langle u, 1 \rangle_{\mathcal{V}} = -\frac{1}{\varepsilon}\langle g(u, \beta), 1 \rangle_{\mathcal{V}} + c \operatorname{vol}(V) = -\frac{1}{\varepsilon}\mathcal{M}(g(u, \beta)) + c \operatorname{vol}(V),$$

where we used that $\mathcal{M}(\Delta u) = 0$. Hence $c = \frac{1}{\varepsilon \operatorname{vol}(V)}\mathcal{M}(g(u, \beta))$ and the mass-conserving Allen–Cahn equation is

$$\frac{du}{dt} = -\Delta u - \frac{1}{\varepsilon} g(u, \beta) + \frac{1}{\varepsilon \operatorname{vol}(V)}\mathcal{M}(g(u, \beta)). \qquad (7.4)$$

We emphasize that c is constant as function in $\mathcal{V}$, that is, it has the same value at each node, but may (and does) depend on u.

We may also impose the fidelity and mass constraints simultaneously. Either by explicit computation of the subdifferential of the sum of the fidelity term and m, or by using the fact that this subdifferential of the sum is equal to the sum of the respective subdifferentials [67, proposition 5.6], we find that the resulting mass-conserving fidelity-forced ($p = 2$) Allen–Cahn equation (version 1) is

$$\frac{du}{dt} = -\Delta u - \frac{1}{\varepsilon} g(u, \beta) - \mu(u - f) + c,$$

for some constant $c \in \mathbb{R}$. As before, we can determine the value of c by requiring that $\langle \frac{du}{dt}, 1 \rangle_{\mathcal{V}} = 0$, which leads to $c = \frac{1}{\mathrm{vol}(V)} \left[\frac{1}{\varepsilon} \mathcal{M}(g(u, \beta)) + \langle \mu, u - f \rangle_{\mathcal{V}} \right]$.

In Calder *et al.* [44] a different approach is taken. Instead of the fidelity term from Section 5.1, a term $-\langle u, \mu f \rangle_{\mathcal{V}}$ is added to the mass-conserving Ginzburg–Landau functional.[49] We note the minus sign. In the minimization of the functional, this term encourages u_i to be large whenever $\mu_i f_i$ is large and to be small whenever $\mu_i f_i$ is small. The corresponding mass-conserving fidelity-forced Allen–Cahn equation (version 2) is

$$\frac{du}{dt} = -\Delta u - \frac{1}{\varepsilon} g(u, \beta) + \mu f + c,$$

where again c is determined by the requirement of mass conservation: $c = \frac{1}{\mathrm{vol}(V)} \left[\frac{1}{\varepsilon} \mathcal{M}(g(u, \beta)) - \langle \mu, f \rangle_{\mathcal{V}} \right]$.

As was the case for the Allen–Cahn equation without constraints (see Remark 7.3), if we use the double-well potential in the constrained equation in (7.3) or (7.4), then the right-hand side of the equation is locally Lipschitz continuous and thus existence and uniqueness of solutions locally in time for any given initial condition follow from the Picard–Lindelöf theorem of ODE theory (see Hale [103, chapter I, theorem 3.1]). A gradient flow argument as in Remark 7.3, this time using the constrained Ginzburg–Landau functionals, again rules out finite-time blowup[50] and thus the solution can be extended to $[0, \infty)$ (see [103, chapter I, theorem 2.1]).

In the double-obstacle potential case (as for (7.2)), we define a solution of (7.3) (or (7.4)) on an interval $T \subseteq \mathbb{R}$ to be a pair $(u, \beta) \in \mathcal{V}_{[0,1], t \in T} \times \mathcal{V}_{t \in T}$ with $u \in H_{\mathrm{loc}}^1(T; \mathcal{V}) \cap C^0(T; \mathcal{V})$ such that (7.3) (or (7.4)) is satisfied at a.e. $t \in T$ and, for all $i \in V$ and a.e. $t \in T$, $\beta_i(t) \in -\partial_{\mathbb{R}_{[0,1]}}(u_i(t))$. (We will sometimes simply refer to u as a solution, implying the existence of a corresponding β.) We refer to Budd and Van Gennip [36, theorems 3.8 and 3.9] and Budd *et al.* [37, theorem 2.7] for proofs of existence and uniqueness of solutions for the initial-value problems corresponding to the mass-constrained and fidelity-forced graph Allen–Cahn equations, respectively. The function u is uniquely determined for all t. In the fidelity-forced case the function β is uniquely determined for a.e.

---

49   In [44] a multiclass functional is used; see Section 11.

50   Alternatively, for solutions of (7.4), we can also use the fact that the (finite) mass of the solution is conserved to rule out finite-time blowup.

t; in the mass-conserving case β is uniquely determined up to a constant for almost every time t. Moreover, this constant is zero if there exists such a time t and a node i such that $u_i(t) \in (0,1)$ (for more details, we refer to [36, theorem 3.8]).

7.4 Different Metrics

A gradient flow is determined by the functional of which the gradient is taken and the metric structure with respect to which the gradient is constructed. Earlier we used the metric induced by the $\mathcal{V}$-inner product. Other choices lead to other gradient flows. In Van Gennip [188, definition 4.1], for example, the H^{-1}-inner product for functions $u, v \in \mathcal{V}$ with $\mathcal{M}(u) = \mathcal{M}(v) = 0$ is introduced:

$$\langle u, v \rangle_{H^{-1}} := \langle \nabla \varphi, \nabla \psi \rangle_{\mathcal{E}} = \langle \Delta \varphi, \psi \rangle_{\mathcal{V}} = \langle \varphi, \Delta \psi \rangle_{\mathcal{V}},$$

where $\varphi, \psi \in \mathcal{V}$ solve the graph Poisson equations $\Delta \varphi = u$ and $\Delta \psi = v$, respectively. In [188, section 3.4] it is proven that the zero-mass conditions on u and v are necessary and sufficient to ensure that these Poisson equations have solutions. Moreover, these solutions are unique up to an additive constant, which does not influence the inner product. In [188, Supplementary Materials section 4] the graph Cahn–Hilliard equation (named thus, in analogy to the continuum H^{-1}-gradient flow of the Ginzburg–Landau functional; see section 3.7.3 in [190]) is derived as the H^{-1}-gradient flow of $\mathrm{GL}_{\varepsilon}$:

$$\frac{du}{dt} = -\Delta \Delta u - \frac{1}{\varepsilon} \Delta (W' \circ u).^{51}$$

Since $\mathcal{M}(\Delta w) = 0$ for any $w \in \mathcal{V}$, we see that the Cahn–Hilliard equation automatically conserves mass. It may appear restrictive that we required u to have zero mass, but if $\mathcal{M}(u) \neq 0$, then we can easily transform u into a function with zero mass: $v = u - \frac{\mathcal{M}(u)}{\mathrm{vol}(V)}$. This addition of a constant (as a function in $\mathcal{V}$) term does not affect the Dirichlet term in $\mathrm{GL}_{\varepsilon}$ and effectively shifts the graph of W (and thus its wells) by $\mathcal{M}(u)/\mathrm{vol}(V)$ to the right. We note that this shift does depend on u, but if we restrict ourselves to functions $u \in \mathcal{V}$ with prescribed mass M (not necessarily zero), we get a constant shift $M/\mathrm{vol}(V)$. This restriction is natural, since the Cahn–Hilliard equation preserves mass.

Other choices for the metric are possible, but have not yet been explored in the literature, to the best current knowledge of the authors.

---

[51] In [188, Supplementary Materials section 4] an extra term appears, because the gradient flow is taken not of $\mathrm{GL}_{\varepsilon}$, but of $\mathrm{GL}_{\varepsilon}$ plus an additional term. Choosing $\gamma = 0$ in [188] returns us to the $\mathrm{GL}_{\varepsilon}$ case. Moreover, an additional factor D^{-r} appears in the potential term in [188], since $\mathcal{W}(u) = \sum_{i \in V} W(u_i)$ is used instead of $\mathcal{W}(u) = \langle W \circ u, 1 \rangle_{\mathcal{V}}$.

8 Merriman–Bence–Osher Scheme

In this section we take a look at a threshold dynamics scheme called the Merriman–Bence–Osher (MBO) scheme.

8.1 Definition of the MBO Scheme

The MBO scheme in the continuum was originally introduced in Merriman *et al.* [146, 147] as a method to approximate the flow by mean curvature (we refer to section 3.7.5 of [190] for more information about continuum mean curvature flow and to Section 9 of this Element for graph variants), but has found its way into the 'differential equations on graphs' literature in recent years mostly as an alternative way to (approximately) minimize GL_ε. Before we consider some reasons why it is not unreasonable to use the scheme for this purpose, we will first give its recursive definition on graphs:

Graph MBO Scheme (without Constraints) ⎯⎯⎯⎯⎯⎯⎯⎯⎯⎯⎯⎯⎯

- **Initialize.** Choose an initial condition $u^0 = \chi_{S_0}$ with $S^0 \subseteq V$ and a 'time step'[52] $\tau > 0$.
- **Step $k+1$: diffusion.** Solve the diffusion/heat equation $\frac{du}{dt} = -\Delta u$ on $(0, \tau]$ with initial condition $u(0) = u^k$.
- **Step $k+1$: threshold.** Define, for all $i \in V$, $u_i^{k+1} := \begin{cases} 0, & \text{if } u_i(\tau) < \frac{1}{2}, \\ 1, & \text{if } u_i(\tau) \geq \frac{1}{2}. \end{cases}$
- **Stop.** Stop the scheme when a stopping condition or predetermined number of steps has been achieved.[53]

By standard methods for linear ODEs (see Hale [103, section III.1]), it follows that the diffusion step has a unique outcome $u(\tau)$, given an initial condition u^k.

The output of this scheme is a sequence of functions $u^0, u^1, u^2, \ldots \in \mathcal{V}_{\{0,1\}}$, or equivalently a sequence of subsets $S^0, S^1, S^2, \ldots \subseteq V$, where $u^k = \chi_{S^k}$. We will freely move between both representations as is convenient.

A potential, minor, source of ambiguity in the literature concerns the value of u_i^{k+1} if $u_i(\tau)$ is exactly at the threshold: if $u_i(\tau) = \frac{1}{2}$, we can decide to set $u^{k+1} = 0$ or $u^{k+1} = 1$. We have decided on the latter for the algorithm given earlier, but in other literature the other choice may have been made. In practice, it is unlikely that $u_i(\tau) = \frac{1}{2}$ is exactly achieved, but for theoretical purposes this choice will determine the (non-)strictness of various inequalities along the way.

---

[52] Also called the diffusion time (step).
[53] For the mathematical analysis of the scheme, it is convenient to assume there is no stopping condition and no upper bound on the number of steps, so that the scheme generates an infinite sequence of output functions u^k.

A first, hand-waving, reason to expect the graph MBO scheme to minimize GL_ε is its superficial similarity to the Allen–Cahn equation from (7.1). Instead of solving a nonlinear differential equation as in (7.1), when executing the MBO scheme the solution of a linear differential equation is sought in the diffusion step up to a, typically small,[54] time $\tau > 0$, after which the phase-separating drive of the W-derived nonlinear term from (7.1) is mimicked by the thresholding step. (For some more details about this interpretation of the MBO scheme as a time-splitting scheme, we refer to remark 6.1.8 in [190].)

Another reason to suspect similar behaviour from the graph MBO scheme as from the graph Allen–Cahn equation is that in the continuum both processes approximate mean curvature flow (for small ε in the Allen–Cahn case and small τ in the MBO case). This can be made rigorous in the form of precisely formulated convergence results, whose details fall outside the scope of the current work. In section 3.7.6 of [190] we give a brief overview of some literature about the continuum versions of the graph models, equations, and schemes we discuss in the current work, including these convergence results.

In chapter 6 of that same work [190], we also present a rigorous link between a specific time discretization of the Allen–Cahn equation with double-obstacle potential (7.2) and the MBO scheme.

8.2 The Signless MBO Scheme

Starting from the signless Ginzburg–Landau functional from Section 5.3, Keetch and Van Gennip [117] and Keetch [116] define a signless MBO scheme.[55]

Signless Graph MBO Scheme _____

- **Initialize (signless).** Choose an initial condition $u^0 = \chi_{S_0} - \chi_{S_0^c}$ with $S^0 \subsetneq V$ and a 'time step' $\tau > 0$.
- **Step $k + 1$: signless diffusion.** Solve the signless diffusion/heat equation $\frac{du}{dt} = -\Delta^\sigma u$ on $(0, \tau]$ with initial condition $u(0) = u^k$.
- **Step $k + 1$: signless threshold.** Define, for all $i \in V$,
$$u_i^{k+1} := \begin{cases} -1, & \text{if } u_i(\tau) < 0, \\ 1, & \text{if } u_i(\tau) \geq 0. \end{cases}$$
- **Stop.**

---

[54] What 'small' exactly means in this context is an interesting topic for study; see, for example, the results on time step selection or freezing (aka pinning) in [33, 35, 36, 37, 124, 173, 187, 191]. See also Section 10.

[55] In [116, 117] the threshold step assigns -1 instead of 1 to nodes i with $u_i(\tau) = 0$. As discussed in Section 8.1, arbitrariness in the choice of value assigned 'at the threshold' is a source of nonuniqueness of definition of these schemes. Here we have kept our choice consistent with that in Section 8.1.

We note that, besides the use of the signless graph Laplacian Δ^σ in the diffusion step, we also require the binary functions[56] u^k to take values that are symmetric with respect to the origin, as argued in Section 5.3.

As with the diffusion step before, standard ODE techniques guarantee the existence of a unique outcome of the signless diffusion step.

In [117] it is shown that the signless MBO scheme performs well for the Max-Cut problem (see Section 5.3) in some practical tests, finding comparable or greater cut values than the Goemans–Williamson algorithm [99], in less computation time – but without any rigorous performance guarantees. Finding such guarantees for any of the MBO-type algorithms is currently still an open question of great interest.

8.3 The MBO Scheme with Constraints

A mass or fidelity constraint, as in Section 5.1, can also be incorporated into the MBO scheme. In the current section we will state and explain these schemes. The rigorous link between the Allen–Cahn equation and MBO scheme which was first established in Budd and Van Gennip [35] and which is also presented in chapter 6 of [190] does explain how these MBO schemes with constraint can be derived from the Allen–Cahn equations with constraint as presented in Section 7.3.

To incorporate a mass constraint as in [188, section 5.3][57] and [36, theorem 4.16], we first require some more notation. If u is the solution of the $(k + 1)^{\text{st}}$ diffusion step, we denote the preimage of $x \in \mathbb{R}$ under u at time τ by

$$U(x) := \{i \in V : u_i(\tau) = x\}.$$

Let $L \in \mathbb{N}$ be the (always strictly positive and finite) number of $x_\ell \in \mathbb{R}$ for which $U(x_\ell) \neq \emptyset$ and assume the labels x_ℓ are such that $x_1 < \ldots < x_L$. Then by [36, theorem 4.16] there is a unique $\ell^* \in [K]$ such that

$$\sum_{\ell=\ell^*+1}^{L} \mathcal{M}(U(x_\ell)) < \mathcal{M}(u^k) \leq \sum_{\ell=\ell^*}^{L} \mathcal{M}(U(x_\ell)).$$

We now replace the threshold step by a mass-conserving threshold step to get a mass-conserving MBO scheme:

---

[56] Sometimes a function which takes two independent variables as input is called a binary function. That is not the sense in which we will use this term. When we refer to a binary function, we mean a function whose image is a subset of a set with two elements, most commonly $\{0, 1\}$ or $\{-1, 1\}$.

[57] We note that the description of the (mcOKMBO) algorithm in [188, section 5.3] contains typos: all instances of '$d_i^r u_i$' in the description at the top of page 2357 should be replaced by 'd_i^r'.

Mass-Conserving Graph MBO Scheme _____

- **Initialize.**
- **Step $k + 1$: diffusion.**
- **Step $k + 1$: mass-conserving threshold.** Let u^{k+1} be any function in $\mathcal{V}$ which satisfies $\mathcal{M}(u^{k+1}) = \mathcal{M}(u^k)$ and, for all $i \in V$,

$$u_i^{k+1} := \begin{cases} 0, & \text{if } u_i(\tau) \in \bigcup_{1 \leq \ell < \ell^*} U(x_\ell), \\ 1, & \text{if } u_i(\tau) \in \bigcup_{\ell^* < \ell \leq L} U(x_\ell). \end{cases}$$

- **Stop.**

Remark 8.1. In the mass-conserving threshold step we order the nodes by their value of the diffused state $u_i(\tau)$ and assign, by setting $u_i^{k+1} = 1$, as much mass to the nodes at the top of the order (with the highest diffused state values $x_L > \ldots > x_{\ell^*+1}$) as we can without assigning more than the required total mass $\mathcal{M}(u_k)$. The leftover mass can be assigned in any way to the nodes in $U(x_{\ell^*})$. If and only if $|U(x_{\ell^*})| > 1$ and $\sum_{\ell=\ell^*}^{L} \mathcal{M}(U(x_\ell)) \neq \mathcal{M}(u^k)$, this introduces nonuniqueness into the scheme (see [36, theorem 4.16] or [33, theorem 4.2.16]). In [188] the choice is made to pick exactly enough (arbitrarily chosen) nodes $i \in U(x_{\ell^*})$ so that all leftover mass can be assigned to them. If $r \neq 0$, the maximum amount of mass that can be assigned per node, namely d_i^r, is node-dependent, so that it is possible (in practice likely) that the leftover mass does not match exactly the sum $\sum d_i^r$ over the chosen nodes. In this case one of the chosen nodes does not get its full mass assigned, that is the resulting function u^{k+1} will be non-binary, since $u_i \notin \{0, 1\}$ at this one node. Other choices to deal with the nonuniqueness are possible, for example, an equal division of mass over all nodes in $U(x_{\ell^*})$, which may also lead to a non-binary function u^{k+1}.

Next, we incorporate a fidelity constraint into the MBO scheme [37], instead of a mass constraint. This time we change the diffusion step of the scheme, instead of the threshold step. Restricting to the case $p = 2$ (i.e., a fidelity term of the form $\frac{1}{2}\|\mu^{\frac{1}{2}}(u-f)\|_{\mathcal{V}}^2$ in the functional) and taking a clue from the fidelity-forced Allen–Cahn equation from (7.3), we replace the diffusion step by a fidelity-forced diffusion step to get a fidelity-forced MBO scheme (version 1):

Fidelity-Forced Graph MBO Scheme (Version 1) _____

- **Initialize.**
- **Step $k + 1$: fidelity-forced diffusion.** Solve the fidelity-forced diffusion/heat equation $\frac{du}{dt} = -\Delta u - \mu(u - f)$ on $(0, \tau]$ with initial condition $u(0) = u^k$.
- **Step $k + 1$: threshold.**
- **Stop.**

The interest in MBO schemes on graphs started with the introduction of this fidelity-forced scheme in Merkurjev *et al.* [144] for classification and image processing applications (see also chapter 4 of [190]).

As before, by the usual methods for linear systems of ODEs (see Hale [103, chapter III.1]), it follows that the fidelity-forced diffusion step has a unique outcome, given an initial condition u^k.

In Section 7.3 we described an alternative way to incorporate a fidelity constraint into a mass-conserving Allen–Cahn equation from Calder *et al.* [44]. This can be used in a non-mass-conserving context as well, giving rise to the following fidelity-forced scheme (version 2) (the continuum limit of which is examined in Laux and Lelmi [124]; see also section 7.2.6 of [190]):

Fidelity-Forced Graph MBO Scheme (Version 2) _____

- **Initialize.**
- **Step $k + 1$: fidelity-forced diffusion.** Solve the fidelity-forced diffusion/heat equation $\frac{du}{dt} = -\Delta u + \mu f$ on $(0, \tau]$ with initial condition $u(0) = u^k$.
- **Step $k + 1$: threshold.**
- **Stop.**

If we impose both a fidelity and mass constraint at once, both the diffusion and threshold steps of the original MBO scheme get replaced. While the threshold step gets replaced by the mass-conserving threshold step as described earlier, the diffusion step must be replaced by a mass-conserving fidelity-forced diffusion step to obtain a mass-conserving fidelity-forced MBO scheme (version 1):

Mass-Conserving Fidelity-Forced Graph MBO Scheme (Version 1) ____

- **Initialize.**
- **Step $k + 1$: mass-conserving fidelity-forced diffusion.** Solve the mass-conserving fidelity-forced diffusion/heat equation $\frac{du}{dt} = -\Delta u - \mu(u - f) + \frac{1}{\text{vol}(V)} \langle \mu, u - f \rangle_V$ on $(0, \tau]$ with initial condition $u(0) = u^k$.
- **Step $k + 1$: mass-conserving threshold.**
- **Stop.**

As above, we can also define a different mass-conserving fidelity-forced MBO scheme, used in Calder *et al.* [44], which uses the following mass-conserving fidelity-forced diffusion step instead of the one described earlier to arrive at a mass-conserving fidelity-forced MBO scheme (version 2):

Mass-Conserving Fidelity-Forced Graph MBO Scheme (Version 2) _____

- **Initialize.**
- **Step $k + 1$: mass-conserving fidelity-forced diffusion.** Solve the mass-conserving fidelity-forced diffusion/heat equation
  $\frac{du}{dt} = -\Delta u + \mu f - \frac{1}{\text{vol}(V)} \langle \mu, f \rangle_V$ on $(0, \tau]$ with initial condition $u(0) = u^k$.
- **Step $k + 1$: mass-conserving threshold.**
- **Stop.**

_____

As for the other diffusion(-like) steps earlier, we note that mass-conserving fidelity-forced diffusion initial-value problems have unique solutions.

As mentioned before, for explanations of how these alternative steps in the MBO scheme can be derived, we refer to [190]. It is also interesting to compare the two alternative fidelity-forced and mass-conserving fidelity-forced MBO schemes which we presented above. A full comparison is an interesting topic for future work. As an initial step, in the companion volume we have included a closer look at the steady states for the two mass-conserving fidelity-forced diffusion steps. It should be noted that in practice these steps will be run for a short time and steady states will not be achieved, but they do shed light on some features that distinguish both methods.

9 Graph Curvature and Mean Curvature Flow

As with many of the other concepts, functionals, and dynamics we have introduced thus far, mean curvature flow (or motion by mean curvature) finds it origins in the continuum setting. It refers to the evolution of a set in which each boundary point moves with a normal velocity proportional to the local mean curvature at that point. In this section we describe various attempts to define a meaningful concept of curvature and mean curvature flow (MCF) on a graph. For some references about mean curvature flow in the continuum setting, we refer to section 3.7.5 of [190]. First we introduce various notions of curvature on graphs.

9.1 Curvature

Various different definitions of graph curvature can be found in the literature. In this section we discuss a few of them.

In the discussion following (3.10) we determined that the maximum in the definition of $TV(u)$ is achieved by $\varphi = \text{sgn}(\nabla u)$. In the continuum setting, if u is the characteristic function of a set with smooth boundary, the supremum in the definition of total variation can be achieved by a smooth extension of the normal vector field on the boundary of the set. Inspired by this, in the graph setting, if u is the characteristic function of some node subset $S \subseteq V$, namely $u = \chi_S$, then we can interpret this edge function φ as a graph normal analogously to the normal vector field in the continuum:

$$v_{ij}^S := (\mathrm{sgn}(\nabla \chi_S))_{ij} = \begin{cases} \mathrm{sgn}\,((\chi_S)_j - (\chi_S)_i), & \text{if } \omega_{ij} > 0, \\ \mathrm{sgn}(0), & \text{if } \omega_{ij} = 0. \end{cases}$$

This prompted Van Gennip *et al.* [191] to define graph (mean) curvature for a node subset S as $\kappa := \mathrm{div}\ v^S$. Thus (allowing for a brief return of our parameter q from (3.1)):

$$\begin{aligned} \kappa_i &= \frac{1}{2} d_i^{-r} \sum_{j \in V} \omega_{ij}^q \left((\mathrm{sgn}(\nabla \chi_S))_{ji} - (\mathrm{sgn}(\nabla \chi_S))_{ij} \right) \\ &= \frac{1}{2} d_i^{-r} \begin{cases} 2 \sum_{j \in S^c} \omega_{ij}^q + \sum_{j \in S} \omega_{ij}^q (\mathrm{sgn}(0) - \mathrm{sgn}(0)), & \text{if } i \in S, \\ -2 \sum_{j \in S} \omega_{ij}^q + \sum_{j \in S^c} \omega_{ij}^q (\mathrm{sgn}(0) - \mathrm{sgn}(0)), & \text{if } i \in S^c, \end{cases} \\ &= d_i^{-r} \begin{cases} \sum_{j \in S^c} \omega_{ij}^q, & \text{if } i \in S, \\ -\sum_{j \in S} \omega_{ij}^q, & \text{if } i \in S^c. \end{cases} \end{aligned}$$

We note that κ is independent of the value chosen for $\mathrm{sgn}(0)$.

In El Bouchairi *et al.* [69, remark 5.1(ii)] the graph mean curvature of a function $u \in \mathcal{V}$ at $i \in V$ is defined as

$$(\mathcal{K}(u))_i := -d_i^{-1} \sum_{j \in V} \omega_{ij}\, \mathrm{sgn}(u_j - u_i), \tag{9.1}$$

where explicitly $\mathrm{sgn}(0) = 1$ is chosen. For $r = 1$ and $q = 1$, $\mathcal{K}(\chi_S)$ would equal κ, if $\mathrm{sgn}(0) = 0$ had been chosen instead. The reason for the choice $\mathrm{sgn}(0) = 1$ in $\mathcal{K}$ is so that $(\mathcal{K}(u))_i$ can be interpreted as the mean curvature $\mathcal{K}_i^{\{j \in V:\, u_j \geq u_i\}}$ of the superlevel set $\{j \in V: u_j \geq u_i\}$ at $i \in V$, where, for $S \subseteq V$ and $i \in V$,

$$\mathcal{K}_i^S := d_i^{-1} \left(\sum_{j \in S^c} \omega_{ij} - \sum_{j \in S} \omega_{ij} \right).$$

We note that $(\mathcal{K}(\chi_S))_i = \begin{cases} \mathcal{K}_i^S, & \text{if } i \in S, \\ -1, & \text{if } i \in S^c. \end{cases}$ The curvature used in El Chakik *et al.* [70] is the same as $\mathcal{K}$ from (9.1).

In Zhou and Schölkopf [206, section 2.4] the authors define the graph mean curvature of $u \in \mathcal{V}$ as

$$-\frac{1}{2} \mathrm{div} \left(\frac{\nabla u}{2 \|\nabla u\|_\varepsilon} \right),$$

where $q = 1$ is chosen in the definition of the $\mathcal{E}$-norm (see (3.1)) and the gradient and divergence operators are scaled to be consistent with the symmetrically normalized Laplacian of (3.6). Aside from the differences in scaling, this approach is similar to the ones mentioned earlier.

Finally we mention two notions of Ricci curvature on graphs: Ollivier's Ricci curvature and Forman's Ricci curvature.

Ollivier curvature (or coarse Ricci curvature; see Ollivier [165, 166], also Münch and Wojciechowski [152]) is defined to be

$$(\kappa_G^O)_{ij} := 1 - \frac{\mathcal{W}_G(\mu_i, \mu_j)}{d_{ij}^G},$$

where $\mu: V \to \mathcal{P}(V)$ assigns a probability measure on the node set V to each node in V[58] and $\mathcal{W}_G$ is a graph Wasserstein distance. In this context, the graph distance d_{ij}^G often is chosen to be as in (3.15) with $q = 2$ (or equivalently $q = 0$, with reciprocal weights) – for unweighted graphs the choice of q in d_{ij}^G is, of course, not relevant.

In Ni *et al.* [162, 163] and Tian *et al.* [185] the probability-measure-valued node function μ is chosen to be

$$\mu_i(j) := \begin{cases} \alpha, & \text{if } j = i, \\ \frac{(1-\alpha)e^{-(d_{ij}^G)^p}}{\sum_{k \in \{j \in V:\, j \sim i\}} e^{-(d_{ik}^G)^p}}, & \text{if } j \sim i, \\ 0, & \text{otherwise,} \end{cases}$$

where, for given $i \in V$, $\mu_i \in \mathcal{P}(V)$ assigns probability $\mu_i(j)$ to node $j \in V$. The parameters $\alpha \in [0,1]$ and $p \geq 0$ are both chosen to be zero for unweighted graphs, in which case the probability distribution μ_i is uniform over the neighbours of i. On random geometric graphs (see section 7.2 of [190]), Van der Hoorn *et al.* [186, section III.B] has a slightly different definition for Ollivier curvature:

$$(\tilde{\kappa}_G^O)_{ij} := 1 - \frac{\mathcal{W}_G(\mu_i, \mu_j)}{\delta},$$

where $\delta > 0$ is the distance between the sample points corresponding to nodes i and j along the geodesic on the manifold from which the points are sampled, and μ_i is the uniform distribution over the set of vertices that are within a weighted graph distance of at most $\delta > 0$ of the node i. If the edge weights ω_{ij} are chosen to be equal to the distance between i and j on the manifold, then in [186], this

---

[58] Here $\mathcal{P}(V)$ denotes the set of probability measures on V, not to be confused with the power set of V, which it denotes in some other, clearly indicated, places in this work.

curvature is proven to converge[59] to the Ricci curvature on the manifold that underlies the random geometric graph. In García Trillos and Weber [96], explicit rates are proved for this convergence. We refer to those papers for further details, such as details about the graph Wasserstein distance (whose explanation would take us a bit too far afield here.) In particular, we refer to [96] for an in-depth discussion of various choices of the graph distance and their impact on the result, and to [186, section II] and the references therein for information about more distinct notions of graph curvature.

Forman curvature (or combinatorial Ricci curvature) is defined in Forman [91] (see also [111, 196, 197]) for cell complexes. Here we do not introduce the concept in this general setting, but rather give its definition applied to graphs. Besides edge weights ω_{ij}, the definition also allows for node weights ω_i. In our standard setting without node weights, we may assume that, for all $i \in V$, $\omega_i = 1$. Forman curvature is then defined to be[60]

$$(\kappa_G^F)_{ij} := \omega_{ij} \left[\frac{\omega_i}{\omega_{ij}} + \frac{\omega_j}{\omega_{ij}} - 2 \sum_{k \in V} \left(\frac{\omega_i}{\sqrt{\omega_{ij}\omega_{ik}}} + \frac{\omega_j}{\sqrt{\omega_{ij}\omega_{kj}}} \right) \right].$$

9.2 Mean Curvature Flow

In Section 9.1 we saw that Van Gennip *et al.* [191] and El Chakik *et al.* [70] introduce very similar notions of graph mean curvature. They also both give definitions of graph MCF, but do so starting from different descriptions of MCF at the continuum level.

In [70] the inspiration comes from the level set description of MCF in the continuum [50, 56, 82, 83, 84, 85]: $\frac{du}{dt} = |\nabla u| \, \text{div} \left(\frac{\nabla u}{|\nabla u|} \right)$, where the operators div and ∇ here denote the continuum versions of the divergence and gradient, respectively. If u satisfies this equation, then each level set of u evolves according to flow by mean curvature. Since $\text{div} \left(\frac{\nabla u}{|\nabla u|} \right)$ gives the curvature of the level sets of u, this leads [70] to introduce the following equations for MCF on graphs:

$$\frac{du_i}{dt} = 2^p (\mathcal{K}(u))_i^+ \|(\nabla u)^+\|_{i,p} - 2^p (\mathcal{K}(u))_i^- \|(\nabla u)^-\|_{i,p}, \qquad \text{if } p \in [1, \infty),$$

$$\frac{du_i}{dt} = (\mathcal{K}(u))_i^+ \|(\nabla u)^+\|_{i,\infty} - (\mathcal{K}(u))_i^- \|(\nabla u)^-\|_{i,\infty}, \qquad \text{if } p = \infty. \quad (9.2)$$

---

[59] Under appropriate conditions, such as the correct scaling of both δ and the connectivity radius (see remark 7.2.4 in [190]) in the random geometric graph with the number of nodes in the graph, and a rescaling of κ_G with δ^{-2}.

[60] The factor 2 in the last term appears if we count (i, j) and (j, i) as different edges; if we identify these edges as the same edge, the factor is 1.

Recall the definitions of the positive and negative parts (superscripts $\pm$) from Remark 3.3. Also recall the node-dependent p-norms from (3.3).

A similar MCF is used in El Bouchairi *et al.* [69] and called power mean curvature flow, where each instance of $\mathcal{K}(u)$ in (9.2) is replaced by $|\mathcal{K}(u)|^{\alpha-1}\mathcal{K}(u)$ for a parameter $\alpha \in [0,1]$ (not to be confused with $\alpha(\varepsilon)$ from Section 5). In particular, if $\alpha = 1$, then [69, formula (6.5)] is the same as (9.2).

If locally in time the mean curvature $(\mathcal{K}(u))_i$ at node i is positive, only the term $2^p(\mathcal{K}(u))_i^+\|(\nabla u)^+\|_{i,p}$ or $(\mathcal{K}(u))_i^+\|(\nabla u)^+\|_{i,\infty}$ remains in the right-hand side of the the the preceding equations, which leads to what [70] calls a discrete dilation process. Similarly, if locally in time the mean curvature $(\mathcal{K}(u))_i < 0$, only the terms with $(\mathcal{K}(u))_i^-$ survive, leading to discrete erosion processes.

To understand those names, we recall from Remark 3.3 that [70, 183] defines (nonlocal) dilation and erosion operators, NLD and NLE, respectively, in terms of the node-dependent ∞-norms. These allow us to rewrite the graph MCF equation in (9.2) for $p = \infty$ as

$$\frac{du_i}{dt} = (\mathcal{K}(u))_i^+ \, (\text{NLD}(u))_i + (\mathcal{K}(u))_i^- \, (\text{NLE}(u))_i - u_i \left[(\mathcal{K}(u))_i^+ + (\mathcal{K}(u))_i^- \right].$$

For further brief discussions of the mean curvature flow from [70], in particular the decrease of total variation along its trajectories, we refer to Budd and Van Gennip [35, remark 6.4] and Budd [33, section 7.5]. Variants of this graph MCF equation are studied in El Bouchairi [68] and El Bouchairi *et al.* [69].

In [191] (we also refer to Van Gennip [187, appendix B.1]) a different, variational, formulation is given for MCF, inspired by the variational formulation for continuum mean curvature flow in Almgren *et al.* [6] and Luckhaus and Sturzenhecker [132]. This is a discrete-in-time scheme generating a sequence of node subsets S^k, starting from an initial set $S^0 \subseteq V$, as follows:

$$S^{k+1} \in \underset{S \subseteq V}{\text{argmin}} \, \text{TV}(\chi_S) + \frac{1}{\delta t}\langle \chi_S - \chi_{S^k}, (\chi_S - \chi_{S^k})d^{\mathfrak{S}^k}\rangle_V. \tag{9.3}$$

Here $d^{\mathfrak{S}^k}$ denotes the graph distance function (see Section 3.3) to $\mathfrak{S}^k$, which is the graph boundary of S^k defined by

$$\mathfrak{S}^k := \{i \in V \colon \exists j \sim i \, (\chi_{S^k})_i \neq (\chi_{S^k})_j\}$$

and $\delta t > 0$ is a time-step parameter.

Besides its cosmetic resemblance to the continuum variational formulation of MCF in [6, 132], the definition for MCF in (9.3) has the desired property that any sequence (S^k) satisfying it does not increase total variation. To be precise, since $S = S^k$ is admissible in the minimization problem in (9.3), we see that

$$\text{TV}(\chi_{S^{k+1}}) \le \text{TV}(\chi_{S^{k+1}}) + \frac{1}{\delta t}\langle \chi_{S^{k+1}} - \chi_{S^k}, (\chi_{S^{k+1}} - \chi_{S^k})d^{\mathfrak{S}^k}\rangle \le \text{TV}(\chi_{S^k}).$$

It is not true, however, that $\text{TV}(\chi_{S^{k+1}}) = \text{TV}(\chi_{S^k})$ only if $S^{k+1} = S^k$. Consider the following counterexample. Let $G = (V, E, \omega)$ be the graph with $V = \{1, 2, 3, 4\}$, $\omega_{12} = \omega_{21} = \omega_{23} = \omega_{32} = \omega_{34} = \omega_{43} = 1$, $\omega_{ij} = 0$ in all other cases, and E contains (i, j) if and only if $\omega_{ij} \ne 0$. If $S^k = \{1, 2\}$, then $\mathfrak{S}^k = \{2, 3\}$ and thus $d_1^{\mathfrak{S}^k} = d_4^{\mathfrak{S}^k} = 1$ and $d_2^{\mathfrak{S}^k} = d_3^{\mathfrak{S}^k} = 0$ (recall from Remark 3.9 that we have chosen $q = 1$). Moreover, $d_1^r = d_4^r = 1$ and $d_2^r = d_3^r = 2^r$. For this example, the second term in the objective function in (9.3) thus becomes

$$\frac{1}{\delta t}\langle \chi_S - \chi_{\{1,2\}}, (\chi_S - \chi_{\{1,2\}})d^{\mathfrak{S}^k}\rangle_V = \frac{1}{\delta t}\left[((\chi_S)_1 - 1)^2 + (\chi_S)_4^2\right].$$

Since $\text{TV}(\chi_{S^k}) = 1$, we know that $\text{TV}(\chi_{S^{k+1}}) \le 1$. Furthermore, if $S \in \{\emptyset, V\}$, then $\text{TV}(\chi_S) = 0$, and if $S \notin \{\emptyset, V\}$, then $\text{TV}(\chi_S) \ge 1$. In the former case, the objective function has value $\frac{1}{\delta t}$. Looking for potential minimizers S in (9.3) that are different from $\emptyset$ and V, we know that $\text{TV}(\chi_S) = 1$, thus $S \in \{\{1\}, \{4\}, \{1, 2\}, \{3, 4\}, \{1, 2, 3\}, \{2, 3, 4\}\}$. Among these candidates, only those that minimize the second term of the objective functional are potential miminizers of (9.3), thus we require $1 \in S$ and $4 \notin S$. This leaves $S \in \{\{1\}, \{1, 2\}, \{1, 2, 3\}\}$. For each of these candidates the objective function has value 1 and thus, if $\delta t < 1$, all these candidates are solutions S^{k+1} of (9.3). In particular we note that two of these candidates are different from S^k, yet $\text{TV}(\chi_{S^{k+1}}) = \text{TV}(\chi_{S^k}) = 1$.

Mean curvature flow of a form very similar to (9.3) is analysed on square grids by Braides *et al.* in [29].

In light of the close connection between the MBO scheme (and the Allen–Cahn equation) and MCF in the continuum that was briefly touched upon in Section 8.1 (and Remark 7.4) – we refer to section 3.7.6 of [190] for more details – a natural question is whether such a connection also exists in the graph setting. In [35, section 6.2] (and in more detail in [33, section 3]) it is argued that a close connection between the graph MBO scheme and the variational graph MCF from (9.3) is not to be expected.

A first reason for this is that, even though when the time step is large (i.e., large τ for MBO and large δt for MCF) each scheme will reach a stationary state equal to $u = 0$ ($S = \emptyset$) or $u = 1$ ($S = V$) after a single time step, the conditions governing which of these two states is chosen are different for MBO and MCF.

Since the main interest in these schemes is at small time steps, this first reason by itself would not necessarily be enough to abandon the formulation of MCF from (9.3). The other reason provided in [33, section 3] is more damning, if our intention is to connect MBO and MCF. Given a graph $G = (V, E, \omega)$ (satisfying the conditions described in Section 3.1) and $\eta > 0$, we can consider the η-completion of G, which we define to be the graph $G^\eta = (V, V^2, \omega^\eta)$, where $\omega_{ij}^\eta = \omega_{ij}$ if $\omega_{ij} > 0$ and $\omega_{ij}^\eta = \eta$ if $i \neq j$ and $\omega_{ij} = 0$. In [33, theorem 7.3.1] it is shown that the difference (in V-norm) between solutions of the heat equation on G and on G^η is bounded by $C_\eta t e^{Ct}$, where $C > 0$ is a constant and $0 < C_\eta = \mathcal{O}(\eta)$ as $\eta \downarrow 0$.[61] Unless in very specific circumstances in which this small difference places both solutions on different sides of the threshold value in the MBO scheme, this shows that the MBO scheme will have very similar, if not the same, solutions on G and G^η. A similar conclusion is shown to hold for solutions of the graph Allen–Cahn equation.[62] On the other hand, however, if $S^k \notin \{\emptyset, V\}$, then the graph boundary $\mathfrak{S}^k$ on G^η is equal to V, thus $d^{\mathfrak{S}^k} = 0$ and (9.3) reduces to $S^{k+1} \in \text{argmin}_{S \subseteq V} \text{TV}(\chi_S) = \{\emptyset, V\}$. For most graphs G, this behaviour of MCF on G^η will differ significantly from the behaviour of MCF (according to (9.3)) on G. In other words, while the behaviour of solutions to the Allen–Cahn equation or MBO scheme is expected to be very stable under the η-completion of G, the behaviour of solutions of (9.3) is not. Simple redefinitions of the graph boundary, for example as $\mathfrak{S}^k \cap S^k$ or $\mathfrak{S}^k \cap (V \setminus S^k)$, do nothing to alter this conclusion.

A promising alternative is offered in [35, section 6.2] and [33, section 7.4]:

$$S^{k+1} \in \underset{S \subseteq V}{\text{argmin}} \, \text{TV}(\chi_S) + \frac{1}{\tau} \| e^{-\frac{1}{2}\tau\Delta}(\chi_S - \chi_{S^k}) \|_V^2. \tag{9.4}$$

Just as we saw for solutions of (9.3), solutions of (9.4) satisfy $\text{TV}(\chi_{S^{k+1}}) \leq \text{TV}(\chi_{S^k})$. Unlike before, we now also have that equality is achieved if and only if $S^{k+1} = S^k$, since $e^{-\frac{1}{2}\tau\Delta}$ is an invertible operator and thus equality in

$$\text{TV}(\chi_{S^{k+1}}) \leq \text{TV}(\chi_{S^{k+1}}) + \frac{1}{\tau} \| e^{-\frac{1}{2}\tau\Delta}(\chi_{S^{k+1}} - \chi_{S^k}) \|_V^2 \leq \text{TV}(\chi_{S^k}).$$

cannot be achieved unless $\chi_{S^{k+1}} - \chi_{S^k} = 0$ [33, proposition 7.4.1].

The main objection against the formulation in (9.3) does not apply to the formulation in (9.4). The total variation term in the objective function in (9.4) depends linearly on the edge weights and thus will differ only by an $\mathcal{O}(\eta)$ term between graphs G and G^η; the second term in the objective function depends on the solution of the graph diffusion equation and thus, by the argument from [33, theorem 7.3.1] discussed earlier, will also only differ by an $\mathcal{O}(\eta)$ term.

---

[61] By this we mean that there exists a $\tilde{C} > 0$ such that, for $\eta > 0$ small enough, $|C_\eta| \leq \tilde{C}\eta$. (See footnote 39.)

[62] Technically, it is only shown for the Allen–Cahn equation with smooth enough potentials, such as the double-well potential. In [33, note 39] it is argued that a similar conclusion holds when the double-obstacle potential is used, except potentially in very pathological circumstances.

The other, minor, objection which was brought against (9.3) also does not apply here. It is argued in [33, section 7.4] that the behaviour at large τ of the scheme in (9.3) is very similar to that of the MBO scheme at large τ.

In section 6.3 of [190] we compare MCF defined by (9.4) more closely with the MBO scheme.

10 Freezing of Allen–Cahn, MBO, and Mean Curvature Flow

Freezing (or pinning) is the phenomenon where for very small values of the parameters ε (in the graph Allen–Cahn equation), τ (in the graph MBO scheme), or δt or τ (in the variational graph mean curvature flow) no, or only trivial, dynamics occur. (See also footnote 54.)

In the graph Allen–Cahn equation, if the parameter ε is very small, the potential term dominates the right-hand side of the equation, leading to dynamics in which each value u_i simply settles into the well of W in which it starts. Rigorous quantitative statements are made in Van Gennip *et al.* [191, theorem 5.3], Budd and Van Gennip [35, remark 4.7], Budd and van Gennip [36, section 3.3], and Budd [33, theorem 3.4.11]. We collect them in the following lemma.

We define ρ_Δ to be the spectral radius of Δ, namely the maximal eigenvalue of Δ. In general, we write ρ_O for the spectral radius of a linear operator $O: V \to V$.

Lemma 10.1. *Let* $W(x) = (x - 1)^2(x + 1)^2$. *Let* $u^0 \in V$ *and let* u *solve*

$$
\begin{cases}
\frac{du_i}{dt} = -(\Delta u)_i - \frac{1}{\varepsilon} d_i^{-r} W'(u_i), & \text{for all } i \in V \text{ and } t > 0, \\
u(0) = u^0.
\end{cases}
$$

Then there exists a $C > 0$ *such that, for all* $t \geq 0$, $\|u(t)\|_V \leq C$. *Now assume additionally that there exists an* $\alpha \in (0, 1)$ *such that, for all* $i \in V$, $|u_i^0| \geq \alpha$. *If*

$$
\varepsilon \leq C^{-1} \rho_\Delta^{-1} 4\alpha(1 - \alpha^2) \left(\max_{i \in V} d_i \right)^{-\frac{r}{2}}, \text{ or}
$$

$$
\varepsilon \leq \left(\sup_{t \geq 0} \|\Delta u(t)\|_{V,\infty} \right)^{-1} 4\alpha(1 - \alpha^2) \left(\max_{i \in V} d_i \right)^{-r},
$$

then, for all $i \in V$, $t \mapsto \operatorname{sgn}(u_i(t))$ *is constant.*

Now assume that W *is the double obstacle potential from* (5.1) *instead and* T *is some interval. Let* S *be a strict and nonempty subset of* V. *Then* $u(t) = \chi_S$, *for all* $t \in T$, *is a solution of* (7.2) *if and only if*

$$
\varepsilon \leq \frac{1}{2} \|\Delta \chi_S\|_{V,\infty}^{-1}.
$$

Similarly $u(t) = \chi_S$ solves the mass-conserving Equation (7.4) if and only if

$$\varepsilon \max_{i \in S^c} |(\Delta \chi_S)_i| \leq 1 - \varepsilon \max_{i \in S} |(\Delta \chi_S)_i|.$$

This latter condition is satisfied if $\varepsilon \leq \frac{1}{2} \|\Delta \chi_S\|_{\mathcal{V},\infty}^{-1}$.

Lastly, $u(t) = \chi_S$ solves the fidelity-forced equation (7.3) if and only if

$$\varepsilon \max_{i \in S^c} (|(\Delta \chi_S)_i| + f_i) \leq \frac{1}{2} \quad and \quad \varepsilon \max_{i \in S} (|(\Delta \chi_S)_i| - f_i + \mu_i) \leq \frac{1}{2}.$$

For the graph MBO scheme, the pinning or freezing phenomenon appears in a different guise. If the time parameter τ in the diffusion step is so small that at every node the local function value does not cross the threshold value, then the thresholding step will return the initial value and hence the scheme is stationary. The critical value of τ below which this behaviour is produced, depends not only on the structure of the graph, but also on the initial condition that is fed into the diffusion step. After all, it is known that for fixed τ the graph MBO schemes converge in a finite number of steps [191, proposition 4.6] and so eventually a stationary state will be reached which, for the given τ, will be 'frozen' by the scheme. In practical applications, however, one wants to choose a value of τ that does not immediately freeze the initial condition that is given at the start of the first iteration of the scheme. The following lemma collects bounds on the critical value for τ for various variants of the graph MBO scheme. These bounds are not sharp and to the best of the authors' knowledge, sharp bounds are not currently known. Similar restrictions on the size of τ were already discussed in the context of a finite-difference discretization of the continuum MBO scheme in Ruuth [173, section 2.3]. The bounds listed in the next lemma are taken from Van Gennip *et al.* [191, theorem 4.2], Budd and Van Gennip [35, theorem 4.5 and remark 4.6], Budd and Van Gennip [36, theorem 4.24] (for the mass-conserving scheme), Budd [33, section 4.3.2] (for both the mass-conserving scheme and the fidelity-forced scheme), Keetch and Van Gennip [117, theorem 5.3] (for the signless scheme), and Keetch [116, theorem 4.2.3] (also for the signless scheme). The references [33, 35, 36] actually provide information about a whole family of schemes, of which graph MBO is only one member. These so-called semidiscrete implicit Euler (SDIE) schemes[63] are the main objects of study in chapter 6 of [190] and we briefly address the topic of freezing then and there.

---

[63] Recently, the authors were made aware that the SDIE scheme may be called an *implicit exponential scheme*. We thank Daniele Avitabile for letting us know. For more details we refer to footnote 210 of [190].

To ease notation, we define $\mathscr{A} : V \to V$ by $\mathscr{A}u := \Delta u + \mu u$. Recall that $\rho_{\mathscr{A}}$ and $\rho_{\Delta^{\sigma}}$ are the spectral radii of $\mathscr{A}$ and the signless Laplacian Δ^{σ}, respectively.

Lemma 10.2. *Let* $k \in \mathbb{N}_0$, $S \subseteq V$ *such that* $\emptyset \neq S \neq V$, *and* $u^k = \chi_S$. *Let* u^{k+1} *be the result of one iteration of either the graph MBO scheme or the mass-conserving graph MBO scheme applied to initial condition* u^k. *If*

$$\tau < \frac{1}{2\|\Delta\chi_S\|_{V,\infty}}$$

or

$$\tau < \rho_{\Delta}^{-1} \log \left(1 + \frac{1}{2} \left(\min_{i \in V} d_i \right)^{r/2} \text{vol}(S)^{-1/2} \right), \tag{10.1}$$

then $u^{k+1} = u^k$.

Alternatively, let $S \subseteq V$ ($S = \emptyset$ *or* $S = V$ *are now allowed) and let* u^{k+1} *be the result of one iteration of the fidelity-forced graph MBO scheme applied to initial condition* u^k. *If*

$$\tau < \frac{1}{2 \sup_{t \in [0,\infty)} \|e^{-t\mathscr{A}} \chi_V\|_{V,\infty} \|\mathscr{A}\chi_S - f\|_{V,\infty}}$$

or

$$\tau < \rho_{\mathscr{A}}^{-1} \log \left(1 + \frac{1}{2} \left(\min_{i \in V} d_i \right)^{r/2} \left(\text{vol}(S)^{1/2} + \rho_{\mathscr{A}}^{-1} \|f\|_V \right)^{-1} \right),$$

then $u^{k+1} = u^k$.

Finally, let $S \subseteq V$ *and* $u^k = \chi_S - \chi_{S^c}$, *and let* u^{k+1} *be the result of one iteration of the signless graph MBO scheme applied to initial condition* u^k. *If*

$$\tau < \rho_{\Delta^{\sigma}}^{-1} \log \left(1 + \left(\min_{i \in V} d_i \right)^{r/2} \text{vol}(V)^{-1/2} \right),$$

then $u^{k+1} = u^k$.

If we let $f = 0$ and $\mathscr{A} = \Delta$ in the fidelity-forced case, we observe that we recover the conditions for the graph MBO scheme without forcing.

We note that the restriction $\emptyset \neq S \neq V$ in the first part of Lemma 10.2, does not diminish the generality of the lemma, since $\chi_{\emptyset}$ and χ_V are stationary states of the (mass-conserving) graph MBO scheme for any $\tau > 0$.

For the signless graph MBO scheme only one condition for τ is given in Lemma 10.2, whereas two conditions are given for the other two schemes. To mimic one of the proofs from the other schemes to try and derive a second condition for the signless scheme, we would require a comparison principle (as in [191, lemma 2.6(d)]; see also [33, theorem 3.2.6]) for the signless graph Laplacian Δ^σ to produce an analogue of the proof of [191, theorem 4.2], or we would require $e^{-t\Delta^\sigma}$ to have a matrix representation with only nonnegative elements to mimic the proof from [33, lemma 4.3.4]. Neither is true; for a counterexample see section 3.4 of [190]. (Of course, the fact that mimicking the proofs from the other schemes does not work, does not prove a similar second condition does not hold.)

Remark 10.3. In section 6.1 [190] we present variational formulations of the graph MBO scheme and its fidelity-forced and mass-conserving variants. The functions generated by these schemes are solutions of these variational problems, but, due to some subtle nonuniqueness issues that are explained in that book, these are not the only solutions. Despite that, the results presented in Lemma 10.1 for these three graph MBO schemes in fact hold for all solutions of their variational formulations.

In [191, theorem 4.8] (with an updated proof in [187, appendix A]) a condition for pinning in the graph MBO scheme *at a specific node* was given that depended only on the local graph structure around that node. Unfortunately, later in [187, theorem 3.1], it was proven that this is an 'empty' condition, namely that it cannot be satisfied by any graph. In [187, sections 4 and 5] 'nonempty' local conditions are provided specifically for star graphs and regular trees.

Pinning occurs in the MBO scheme if τ is chosen to be small; on the other hand, if τ is large, another example of trivial dynamics may occur, as one implementation of the diffusion step could lead to a state $u(\tau)$ which is close to the constant steady state $\frac{M(u^0)}{\text{vol}(V)}\chi_V$ and hence the subsequent threshold step would return either $u^1 = \chi_V$ or $u^1 = \chi_\emptyset$, which are stationary states of the MBO scheme. The following lemma gives a precise result (originally published as [191, theorem 4.3]). We write λ_2 for the second smallest eigenvalue of Δ (i.e., the algebraic connectivity; see Section 6).[64]

Lemma 10.4. *Let $k \in \mathbb{N}_0$, $S \subseteq V$, $u^k = \chi_S$, and assume that $R_S := \frac{M(u^k)}{\text{vol}(V)} \neq \frac{1}{2}$. Let u^{k+1} be the result of one iteration of the graph MBO scheme applied to initial condition u^k. If*

$$\tau > \lambda_2^{-1} \log\left(\frac{(\text{vol}(S))^{1/2}(\text{vol}(S^c))^{1/2}}{(\text{vol}(V))^{1/2}|R_S - \frac{1}{2}|(\min_{i\in V} d_i)^{r/2}}\right), \tag{10.2}$$

---

[64] We recall from Lemma 6.1 that the smallest eigenvalue is zero and, since we are working with a connected graph, $\lambda_2 > 0$.

then

$$u^{k+1} = \begin{cases} \chi_V, & \text{if } R_S > \frac{1}{2}, \\ \chi_\emptyset, & \text{if } R_S < \frac{1}{2}. \end{cases}$$

It is natural to ask if there is a gap between the lower bound of (10.1) below which pinning occurs in the MBO scheme and the upper bound of (10.2) above which the dynamics is trivial in the way described in Lemma 10.4. The following result from [191, theorem 4.4] (with corrections to the proof in [187, appendix B.2]; see also the discussion in [33, section 7.3.2]) answers affirmatively.

Lemma 10.5. *If* $\frac{\lambda_2}{\rho_\Delta} < \frac{\log \sqrt{2}}{\log(3/2)} \approx 0.85$, *then there exists a* τ *which does satisfy neither the inequality in* (10.1), *nor the inequality in* (10.2).

We emphasize that there is no reason to believe that the inequality conditions in the lemmas above are sharp. In particular, Lemma 10.5 does not preclude the possibility that, for a particular given graph and particular given initial condition u^k, every choice of $\tau > 0$ leads to either the behaviour described in Lemma 10.2 or the behaviour from Lemma 10.4.

In Boyd *et al.* [27, propositions 4.1 and 4.2], results similar to some of those in Lemmas 10.2 and 10.4 are presented for an MBO scheme with a generalized diffusion step.[65] That particular scheme is used for modularity optimization (see section 4.1.4 of [190]). The practical suggestion in [27, section 4.5] is to choose τ as the geometric mean of the (trivial-dynamics-avoiding) upper and lower bounds that are obtained for τ.

We end this section by taking a brief look at the behaviour of graph mean curvature flow for small τ and large τ. As explained in Section 9.2 there is currently not one main definition for the graph MCF and the behaviour at small or large time steps will depend on which form of the scheme that is chosen. For some notes on the small time-step behaviour of some of the variational graph MCF formulations we refer the interested reader to [191, remark 3.10] and [33, theorem 7.4.2 and note 38], for information about behaviour at large time steps to [33, sections 7.3.2 and 7.4]. We end this section by giving some results from [33, section 7.4] for the graph MCF defined in (9.4) in detail.

We require the Lambert W-function [57], which we denote by W_L. We note that, if $x \in [0, \infty)$ (as is the relevant case in Lemma 10.6), then W_L is the unique function on $[0, \infty)$ that satisfies $W_L(x)e^{W_L(x)} = x$. To make the following bound

---

[65] In the notation of [27], for $\gamma = 0$ the scheme of Boyd *et al.* is the same as the graph MBO scheme (without constraints) from Section 8.1 with the combinatorial graph Laplacian.

more intuitive, we note the following simple approximation for $W_L(x)$ when $x \geq 0$, which is given in Iacono and Boyd [107]:

$$W_L(x) \approx \log\left(1 + \frac{x}{1 + \frac{1}{2}\log(1 + x)}\right).$$

Lemma 10.6. *Let $k \in \mathbb{N}$, $S^k \subseteq V$, and let S^{k+1} be a graph MCF update defined by (9.4). If*

$$\tau e^{\tau \rho_\Delta} < \frac{\min_{i \in V} d_i^r}{\max_{S \subseteq V} \mathrm{TV}(\chi_S)}, \text{ or equivalently, } \tau < \rho_\Delta^{-1} W_L\left(\frac{\rho_\Delta \min_{i \in V} d_i^r}{\max_{S \subseteq V} \mathrm{TV}(\chi_S)}\right),$$

then $S^{k+1} = S^k$.

Now assume $\tau > \frac{\mathrm{vol}(V)}{\min_{(i,j) \in E} \omega_{ij}}$, then $S^{k+1} \in \{\emptyset, V\}$. If $\mathrm{vol}(S^k) < \frac{1}{2}\mathrm{vol}(V)$, then $S^{k+1} = \emptyset$. Alternatively, if $\mathrm{vol}(S^k) > \frac{1}{2}\mathrm{vol}(V)$ instead, then $S^{k+1} = V$.

We note that the volume conditions on S^k in the 'large τ' case of Lemma 10.6, correspond to the conditions on R_S in Lemma 10.4 which decided the 'large τ' behaviour of the MBO scheme.

The results we have mentioned thus far have all been obtained by studying the discrete schemes directly and all provide parameter regions in which freezing is guaranteed to happen. A different approach is to consider the continuum limit of the graph-based MBO scheme and obtain parameter scalings under which the limiting dynamics is not frozen, as a way to guide parameter choices to avoid freezing. One example in the literature is Misiats and Yip [149], which considers three regimes for the parameter τ for MBO on a two-dimensional square grid with grid size h. With $h = C(\tau)^\gamma$, for some constant $C > 0$, the regimes are $\gamma > 1$, in which the limiting dynamics is mean curvature flow; $\gamma < 1$, in which the limiting dynamics is frozen; and the critical case $\gamma = 1$ in which the dynamics depends on finer details. Another example is Laux and Lelmi [124, theorem 6 and corollary 8] which studies the continuum limit of (a generalization of) the graph MBO scheme on random geometric graphs and guarantees nontrivial limit dynamics if $\tau \downarrow 0$ such that $\lim_{|V| \to \infty}[(\log(|V|))^\alpha \tau]^{-1} = 0$ and $\lim_{|V| \to \infty} \varepsilon(\log(|V|))^\beta = 0$, for constants $\alpha > 0$ (not to be confused with $\alpha(\varepsilon)$ from Section 5) and $\beta > 0$ in a specified range. Here ε is the length scale used to construct the edge weights in the graph. (More details about the construction of the random geometric graphs are given in section 7.2 of [190].) Interestingly, the convergence to limiting dynamics remains valid even if the spectral decomposition of the graph Laplacian is truncated after the lowest K eigenvalues and their corresponding eigenfunctions, as is commonly done in implementations to keep the scheme computationally manageable and to filter out noise that may be present in the higher eigenfunctions (see also chapter 5 [190]). In this case $K \geq (\log(|V|))^q$ is required, for $q > 0$ (unrelated to the parameter q from Section 3) in a specified range.

11 Multiclass Extensions

The models we have discussed so far all describe exactly two phases (or classes, or clusters), which allows for a characterization of the state of the system via a single (approximately) binary-valued function u. Many of these models can be extended to incorporate multiple classes; in this section we will discuss some of these extensions, specifically for the Ginzburg–Landau functional, Allen–Cahn equation, and MBO scheme. (In Shen and Kang [175] total variation for functions on a continuum domain and with a discrete multiclass range (*quantum TV*) is investigated for image processing applications.)

The two-phase nature of the functional GL_ε is the result of the double-well potential and double-obstacle potential each achieving their minimum value in two places ('wells'). For a multiphase version of the Ginzburg–Landau functional, we thus require a potential with multiple minimizers.

One approach is using a potential function $\tilde{W} \colon \mathbb{R} \to \mathbb{R}$ with multiple wells instead of W, as is done with a periodic-well potential in Garcia-Cardona *et al.* [93, 94]. The one-dimensional domain of $\tilde{W}$ has the advantage that the state of the system can still be described by a single real-valued function $u \colon V \to \mathbb{R}$; but having more than two wells in the one-dimensional domain necessarily creates an asymmetry in the distances between the wells. For example, if the potential has wells located at -1, 0, and 1, then the distance between the first and third wells is twice that between the first and second wells. Combined with the Dirichlet energy term in the Ginzburg–Landau functional, this creates an unwanted bias in favour of interfaces between the -1- and 0-phases (or between the 0- and 1-phases) over interfaces between the -1- and 1-phases. In [93, 94] this problem is resolved by the use of a generalized difference function in the Dirichlet energy term, which compensates for the asymmetry.

A second approach, which has found more traction in the literature, is using a potential function on a higher-dimensional domain, as in Merkurjev *et al.* [143] and Garcia-Cardona *et al.* [95]. The state of a system with K phases is now described by a vector-valued function $u \colon V \to \mathbb{R}^K$. We denote the set of such functions by $\mathcal{V}^K := \mathcal{V}_{\mathbb{R}^K}$ and the kth component of the value of such a function u at node i by $(u_i)_k \in \mathbb{R}$. Just as there is a bijective correspondence between functions $u \in \mathcal{V}$ and vectors in $\mathbb{R}^n$ (see Remark 3.4), there is also a bijective correspondence between functions $u \in \mathcal{V}^K$ and n-by-K real matrices U, with entries $U_{ij} = (u_i)_j$, that is, U_{ij} is the jth entry of the vector $u_i \in \mathbb{R}^K$. We write $u_{\cdot j}$ for the jth component function of u, that is, $(u_{\cdot j})_i = (u_i)_j$. The K phases are represented by the standard basis vectors[66] $e_k \in \mathbb{R}^K$ (i.e., $(e_k)_j = 1$ if $k = j$ and $(e_k)_j = 0$ if $k \neq j$), with $k \in [K]$, and thus the potential function should have wells located at the corners of the K-dimensional Gibbs simplex

$$\Sigma^K := \left\{ x \in [0,1]^K : \sum_{k=1}^K x_k = 1 \right\}. \tag{11.1}$$

If $E_K := \{e_1, \ldots, e_K\}$ is the set of standard basis vectors in $\mathbb{R}^K$, then

$$\mathcal{V}_E^K := \mathcal{V}_{E_K}$$

is the set of node functions that take values on the corners of the simplex. Hence, if $u \in \mathcal{V}_E^K$ with matrix representation $U \in \mathbb{R}^{n \times K}$ and we write U_{i*} for the ith row of U, then, for all $i \in [n]$, $U_{i*} \in E_K$.

In [95, 143] the multiclass potential

$$W_K(x) := \frac{1}{2} \prod_{k=1}^K \frac{1}{4} \|x - e_k\|_1^2$$

is used for $x \in \mathbb{R}^K$, where $\|x\|_1 := \sum_{i=1}^K |x_i|$ and, more generally, $\|x\|_p := \left(\sum_{i=1}^K |x_i|^p \right)^{\frac{1}{p}}$ for $p \in [1, \infty)$ and $x \in \mathbb{R}^K$. The Dirichlet energy term now extends straightforwardly to K classes:[67]

$$\frac{1}{2} \sum_{k=1}^K \|\nabla u_{\cdot k}\|_{\mathcal{E}}^2,$$

where in matrix representation $u_{\cdot k}$ is represented by the kth column of U. Applying these multiclass extensions to the graph Ginzburg–Landau functional from Section 5, we arrive at the following multiclass graph Ginzburg–Landau functional $\mathrm{GL}_\varepsilon^K : \mathcal{V}^K \to \mathbb{R}$:

$$\mathrm{GL}_\varepsilon^K(u) := \frac{1}{2}\alpha(\varepsilon) \sum_{k=1}^K \|\nabla u_{\cdot k}\|_{\mathcal{E}}^2 + \frac{1}{\varepsilon} \mathcal{W}_K(u),$$

where $\mathcal{W}_K(u) := \sum_{i \in V} W_K(u_i)$ or $\mathcal{W}_K(u) := \sum_{i \in V} d_i^r W_K(u_i)$ (see Section 5 for a discussion about these two options in the context of the two-phase functional GL_ε and about $\alpha(\varepsilon)$; also see Remark 7.1).

---

[66] In machine learning, there is the related notion of *one-hot encoding* of categorical variables: if data point i belongs to category j, then this can be encoded in a matrix U with $U_{ij} = 1$. In our context each data point belongs to one and only one phase, in which case the one-hot encoded rows of U are corners of a Gibbs simplex (see (11.1)). In a more general setting in which a data point can belong to multiple categories, one-hot encoded rows can contain multiple ones.

[67] In [95, 143] the symmetrically normalized Laplacian Δ^{sym} from (3.6) is used instead of Δ in the Dirichlet energy, which can be written in the form $\frac{1}{2} \sum_{k=1}^K \langle u_{\cdot k}, \Delta^{\text{sym}} u_{\cdot k} \rangle_{\mathcal{V}}$.

In the case when $K = 2$, $\mathrm{GL}_\varepsilon^K$ is not equal to GL_ε. We can, however, derive a connection between the two under the assumption that $u_{.1} = v$ and $u_{.2} = 1 - v$, for some $v \in \mathcal{V}$. We note that this is equivalent to requiring $u \in \Sigma^2$, and note that that node i being in one of the pure phases, namely $u_i = e_1 \in \mathbb{R}^2$ or $u_i = e_2 \in \mathbb{R}^2$, corresponds to $v_i = 1$ or $v_i = 0$, respectively. Then we compute

$$\frac{1}{2}\left(\|\nabla u_{.1}\|_\varepsilon^2 + \|\nabla u_{.2}\|_\varepsilon^2\right) = \frac{1}{2}\left(\|\nabla v\|_\varepsilon^2 + \|\nabla(1-v)\|_\varepsilon^2\right) = \|\nabla v\|_\varepsilon^2$$

and

$$W_2(u_i) = \frac{1}{32}\|u_i - e_1\|_1^2\,\|u_i - e_2\|_1^2 = \frac{1}{32}(2|1-v_i|)^2\,(2|v_i|)^2 = 2W(v_i),$$

if $W(x) = \frac{1}{4}x^2(x-1)^2$, which is one of the options discussed in Section 5. Hence, under these assumptions,

$$\mathrm{GL}_\varepsilon^2(u) = 2\,\mathrm{GL}_\varepsilon(v),$$

and so for minimization purposes both functionals are equivalent.

Given a multiclass graph Ginzburg–Landau functional, a corresponding multiclass graph Allen–Cahn equation is defined as its gradient flow with respect to the $\mathcal{V}^K$-inner product

$$\langle u, v \rangle_{\mathcal{V}^K} := \sum_{k=1}^{K} \langle u_{.k}, v_{.k} \rangle_\mathcal{V},$$

for $u, v \in \mathcal{V}^K$. With $s \in \mathbb{R}$ and for all $u, v \in \mathcal{V}^K$, we have

$$\frac{d}{ds}\,\mathrm{GL}_\varepsilon^K(u)\Big|_{s=0} = \alpha(\varepsilon)\langle \overline{\Delta} u, v \rangle_{\mathcal{V}^K} + \frac{1}{\varepsilon}\langle \mathcal{D}W_K \circ u, v \rangle_{\mathcal{V}^K},$$

where $\overline{\Delta} \colon \mathcal{V}^K \to \mathcal{V}^K$ and $\mathcal{D}W_K \colon \mathcal{V}^K \to \mathcal{V}^K$ are defined by, for all $u \in \mathcal{V}^K$, $i \in V$, and $k \in [K]$,

$$\left(\left(\overline{\Delta} u\right)_i\right)_k := (\Delta u_{.k})_i \quad \text{and} \quad ((\mathcal{D}W_K \circ u)_i)_k := \partial_k W_K(u_i),$$

with ∂_k the partial derivative with respect to the kth component of the independent variable in $\mathbb{R}^K$. Here we have chosen $\mathcal{W}_K(u) := \sum_{i \in V} d_i^r W_K(u_i)$; if $\mathcal{W}_K(u) := \sum_{i \in V} W_K(u_i)$ instead, we would need to include the degrees in the second term, as in Remark 7.1, or, equivalently, redefine $((\mathcal{D}W_K(u))_i)_k := d_i^{-r}\partial_k W_K(u_i)$.

This leads to the following multiclass graph Allen–Cahn equation:

$$\frac{du}{dt} = -\alpha(\varepsilon)\overline{\Delta} u - \frac{1}{\varepsilon}\mathcal{D}W_K \circ u.$$

In [95, 143] also a fidelity-forcing term is included in the Allen–Cahn equation.

Similarly, also a multiclass MBO scheme can be defined. In the diffusion step K uncoupled diffusion equations are solved, leading to an intermediate output $u \in \mathcal{V}^K$. In the threshold step, we first project each $u_i \in \mathbb{R}^K$ onto the simplex Σ^K and then assign (one of) the closest corner(s) of the simplex to each node i. This leads to the following scheme.

Multiclass Graph MBO Scheme _____

- **Initialize (multiclass).** Choose an initial condition $u^0 \in \mathcal{V}_E^K$, and $\tau > 0$.
- **Step $l + 1$: multiclass diffusion.** Solve the multiclass diffusion/heat equations: for all $k \in [K]$, $\frac{du_{.k}}{dt} = -\Delta u_{.k}$ on $(0, \tau]$ with initial condition $u(0) = u^l$.
- **Step $l + 1$: multiclass threshold.** For all $i \in V$, define $u_i^{l+1} := e_{k^*} \in \mathbb{R}^K$, where $k^* \in \mathrm{argmin}_{k \in [K]} \|v_i - e_k\|_2$ (if k^* is not unique, a k is chosen uniformly at random out of all minimizers) with $v_i := \mathrm{argmin}_{x \in \Sigma^K} \|u_i - x\|_2.$[68]
- **Stop.**

_____

The initial condition u^0 and the output u^{l+1} of each iteration are functions in $\mathcal{V}_E^K$ and can be interpreted as indicator functions for the K classes: for $k \in [K]$, define $S_k^l := \{i \in V : u_i^l = e_k\}$, then $u_{.k}^l = \chi_{S_k^l}$. The diffusion step thus consists of K uncoupled instances of the standard (i.e., 2-phase) MBO scheme diffusion step, one for each of the K classes. In Cucuringu *et al.* [60, appendix A.3] it is shown that the multiclass threshold step is equivalent to assigning $u_i^{l+1} := e^{k^*}$ where $k^* \in \mathrm{argmax}_{k \in [K]}(u_i)_k$. In other words, the diffusion step is followed by a 'majority vote' determining to which class each node gets assigned.

In Bresson *et al.* [31] a variant of graph multiclass MBO is presented, with a slightly different random-walk-based diffusion step, but more importantly with an incremental reseeding step between iterations: each iteration the initial condition of the diffusion step is created by randomly sampling nodes from each class based on the output of the previous iteration's multiclass threshold step. The number of sampled nodes per class is increased in each iteration.

The ideas presented earlier for the multiclass graph MBO scheme can directly be transferred to the signless setting from Sections 5.3 and 8.2 (see Keetch [116, chapter 5]) and to the fidelity-forced setting [95, 143].

In the signless case we need to take care to replace the standard simplex by

$$\Sigma_{\pm}^K := \left\{ x \in [-1, 1]^K : \sum_{k=1}^{K} x_k = 2 - K \right\},$$

_____

[68] Existence and uniqueness of v_i follow from a well-known result; see, for example, Bagirov *et al.* [14, lemma 2.2].

with corners $E_K^\pm := \{e_1^\pm, \ldots, e_K^\pm\}$, where, for all $i, k \in [K]$, $(e_k^\pm)_i = 1$ if $i = k$ and $(e_k^\pm)_i = -1$ if $i \neq k$. Let $\mathcal{V}_{E^\pm}^K := \mathcal{V}_{E_K^\pm}$ be the set of node-functions with values on the corners of $\Sigma_\pm^K$.

Signless Multiclass Graph MBO Scheme _____

- **Initialize (signless multiclass).** Choose $u^0 \in \mathcal{V}_{E^\pm}^K$ and $\tau > 0$.
- **Step $l + 1$: signless multiclass diffusion.** Solve the multiclass signless diffusion/heat equations: for all $k \in [K]$, $\frac{du_{\cdot k}}{dt} = -\Delta^\sigma u_{\cdot k}$ on $(0, \tau]$; $u(0) = u^l$.
- **Step $l + 1$: signless multiclass threshold.** For all $i \in V$, define $u_i^{l+1} := e_{k^*}^\pm \in \mathbb{R}^K$, where $k^* \in \operatorname{argmin}_{k \in [K]} \|v_i - e_k\|_2$ (if k^* is not unique, a k is chosen uniformly at random out of all minimizers) with $v_i := \operatorname{argmin}_{x \in \Sigma_\pm^K} \|u_i - x\|_2$.[69]
- **Stop.**

_____

We again refer to [60, appendix A.3] for a 'majority vote' interpretation of the signless multiclass threshold step.

For the multiclass fidelity-forced MBO scheme, we need multiclass versions of the fidelity parameter function μ and reference function f from Section 5.1; that is, $\mu \in \mathcal{V}_{[0,\infty)^K} \setminus \{0\}$[70] and $f \in \mathcal{V}^K$. In [95, 143] each $\mu_{\cdot k}$ is chosen to be the same and f is chosen from $\mathcal{V}_E^K$.

Multiclass Fidelity-Forced Graph MBO Scheme _____

- **Initialize (multiclass).**
- **Step $l + 1$: multiclass fidelity-forced diffusion.** Solve the multiclass fidelity-forced diffusion/heat equations: for all $k \in [K]$, $\frac{du_{\cdot k}}{dt} = -\Delta u_{\cdot k} - \mu_{\cdot k}(u_{\cdot k} - f_{\cdot k})$ on $(0, \tau]$ with initial condition $u(0) = u^l$.
- **Step $l + 1$: multiclass threshold.**
- **Stop.**

_____

A multiclass mass-conserving graph MBO scheme called auction dynamics is developed in Jacobs *et al.* [110] (for $r = 0$), based on the (unconstrained) *continuum* multiclass MBO scheme that was introduced in Esedoğlu and Otto [77] to approximate multiclass mean curvature flow. The mass of each class is specified, that is, for a given $M \in \mathbb{R}^K$ it is imposed that, for all $k \in [K]$, $\mathcal{M}(u_{\cdot k}) = M_k$. In order that the mass is conserved, the simple majority vote from the multiclass threshold step has to be adapted by a class-dependent correction term p_k. (Approximately) determining this term is accomplished in [110] via the duality theory of linear programming. The name 'auction dynamics' is inspired by an interpretation of the scheme in which each node is bidding

_____

[69] As in footnote 68, existence and uniqueness of v_i follow from, for example, Bagirov *et al.* [14, lemma 2.2].
[70] If fidelity-forcing is required in each of the K classes, then each $\mu_{\cdot k}$ should be non-zero.

for membership of one of the K classes, with $u_i \in \mathbb{R}^K$ the vector of weighted preferences of node i for each class and p_k the price of membership for class k. For details we refer to [110].

At the time of writing and to the best knowledge of the authors, it is an open question whether this auction dynamics scheme can also be derived starting from a multiclass mass-conserving Allen–Cahn equation similar to the way the binary mass-conserving MBO scheme from Section 8.3 is derived as explained in section 6.1.2 of [190].

In [110] auction dynamics is also extended to handle upper and lower bounds on the masses of the classes, rather than exactly prescribed masses.

In the context of Poisson learning (see Section 12) Calder *et al.* [44] implement a multiclass version of the mass-conserving fidelity-forced graph MBO scheme (version 2) from Section 8.3, which they name PoissonMBO and which takes the following form.[71]

Multiclass Mass-Conserving Fidelity-Forced Graph MBO Scheme _____

- **Initialize (multiclass).**
- **Step $l+1$: multiclass mass-conserving fidelity-forced diffusion.** Solve the multiclass mass-conserving fidelity-forced diffusion/heat equations: for all $k \in [K]$, $\frac{du_{\cdot k}}{dt} = -\Delta u_{\cdot k} + \mu_{\cdot k} f_{\cdot k} - \langle \mu_{\cdot k}, f_{\cdot k} \rangle_{\mathcal{V}}$ on $(0, \tau]$, with $u(0) = u^l$.
- **Step $l + 1$: multiclass mass-conserving threshold.** For all $i \in V$, define $u_i^{l+1} := e_{k^*} \in \mathbb{R}^K$, where $k^* \in \mathrm{argmin}_{k \in [K]} \| v_i - e_k \|_2$ (in case of nonuniqueness of minimizers one k is chosen uniformly at random out of all minimizers) with $v_i := \sum_{k=1}^{K} c_k (u_i)_k$, where the strictly positive constants c_k are chosen such that, for all $k \in [K]$, $\mathcal{M}(u_{\cdot k}) = \mathcal{M}(u_{\cdot k}^0)$.
- **Stop.**

It is argued in [44, remark 2.2] that the constants $c_k > 0$ in the multiclass mass-conserving threshold step can always be chosen such that the mass constraints are satisfied.

In section 7.2.6 of [190] some further multiclass MBO schemes and their continuum limits are discussed.

12 Laplacian Learning and Poisson Learning

A function $u \in \mathcal{V}$ is *harmonic* at $i \in V$, if $(\Delta u)_i = 0$. In Zhu *et al.* [211] the random walk graph Laplacian ($r = 1$) is used, but other Laplacians appear in the literature as well. If $S \subseteq V$ and u is harmonic at all $i \in V \setminus S$, then u is said to be harmonic on $V \setminus S$. If $S \neq \emptyset$ and $\tilde{f}: S \to \mathbb{R}$ is given, there exists a

---

[71] To be consistent with the other MBO schemes, we write f for the $\tilde{f}$ of Section 8.3.

unique function $u \in \mathcal{V}$ such that u is harmonic on $V \setminus S$ and $u|_S = \tilde{f}$, see Lovász [130, theorem 3.1.2]. This is called the *harmonic extension* of f. For introductory notes on harmonic functions on graphs, see Wigderson [199]. In [211] this harmonic extension of $\tilde{f}$ is suggested as a good candidate for semi-supervised learning (we refer to section 4.1.2 of [190] for more information about semi-supervised learning) of binary labels on a graph (*label propagation*), given the a priori labels $\tilde{f}$ on S. This technique is called *Laplacian learning* (or Laplace learning). In Zhu *et al.* [210] the harmonic extension is interpreted as the mean of an associated Gaussian Random Field. To go from the real-valued harmonic extension $\tilde{f}$ to binary labels, simple thresholding suffices – or mass-conserving thresholding if the preferred cluster sizes are known – in the vein of the MBO scheme(s) of Section 11. Extensions to multiple labels are also possible, similar to the multiclass extension of Calder *et al.* [44] which we discuss in Section 11.

The Laplacian learning problem

$$\begin{cases} \Delta \tilde{u} = 0, & \text{on } V \setminus S, \\ \tilde{u} = \tilde{f}, & \text{on } S, \end{cases} \tag{12.1}$$

can be transformed, via $u := \tilde{u} - f$, where

$$f := \begin{cases} 0, & \text{on } V \setminus S, \\ \tilde{f}, & \text{on } S, \end{cases} \tag{12.2}$$

to the *semihomogeneous Dirichlet problem*

$$\begin{cases} \Delta u = -\Delta f, & \text{on } V \setminus S, \\ u = 0, & \text{on } S. \end{cases}$$

The unique solution to this problem can be constructed in terms of a *Green's function* [53, 54], which itself can be expressed in terms of *equilibrium measures* [19, 188] (see also appendix B of [190]).

The Laplacian learning problem in (12.1) also has a variational formulation.

Lemma 12.1. *Let $u \in \mathcal{V}$, then u is the unique solution of (12.1) if and only if*

$$u \in \operatorname*{argmin}_{\hat{u} \in \mathcal{V}} \|\nabla \hat{u}\|_{\mathcal{E}}^2 \quad \text{s.t.} \quad \hat{u}|_S = \tilde{f}. \tag{12.3}$$

Proof. For a proof, we refer to lemma 3.5.1 in [190]. □

Laplacian learning and variants (often using the Dirichlet energy as a regularizer in a variational setting, inspired by (12.3)), have been applied in various settings, for example in Zhou and Schölkopf [206], Zhou *et al.* [204], and Elmoataz *et al.* [74]. One generalization is the *p*-Laplacian learning problem (see [206]) which uses $\|\nabla u\|_{\mathcal{E},p}^p$ in (12.3) instead of $\|\nabla u\|_{\mathcal{E}}^2$.[72] However, when there are many a priori unlabelled nodes (i.e., when $|V \setminus S|$ is large), there are some drawbacks. In particular, for random geometric graphs built from point clouds in $\mathbb{R}^d$ it has been shown that when $|S|$ is fixed and $p \leq d$, solutions to the limiting problem $|V \setminus S| \to \infty$ are relatively flat, except for spikes concentrated around the a priori labelled points (see, e.g., [208]). When $p > d$, solutions to the limiting problem do not exhibit this unwanted behaviour, assuming the length scale in the edge weight function (which regulates the strength of the connection between points in the point cloud based on their Euclidean distance) decreases slowly enough as $|V \setminus S| \to \infty$. For technical details, we refer to Slepčev and Thorpe [179]; see also [4, section 7.2]. In Crook *et al.* [59] this connection to the limiting problem is exploited to develop a new numerical method for solving p-Laplacian learning. In Calder *et al.* [44] this degeneracy issue for $p = 2$ is related to the random walk interpretation of Laplace learning, in which u_i equals the expected value of $\tilde{f}_j$, where $j \in S$ is the first node in S that a random walk starting from node i hits.[73] Also for $p = 2$, Calder and Slepčev in [43] address this degeneracy issue by adapting the weights of edges that connect to nodes (i.e., points in the point cloud) that are near to the a priori labelled points.

When $p = \infty$, ∞-Laplacian learning is also called Lipschitz learning, see Kyng *et al.* [123]. Various graph-to-continuum consistency results for Lipschitz learning, as well as learning with the game-theoretic p-Laplacian from (3.14) (or variants thereof) are established in, for example, Flores *et al.* [90] (for more literature references, see section 3.5 of [190]).

In Weihs and Thorpe [198], fractional-Laplacian learning is studied (especially its consistency at the variational level; we refer to section 7.4 of [190]), which is based on another variant of the graph Dirichlet energy:

$$\langle u, \Delta^s u \rangle_{\mathcal{V}},$$

with parameter $s > 0$ (and $r = 0$ in Δ).

Another variant is Poisson learning, which is suggested in [44] as a way to avoid the degeneracy issue that we discussed earlier:

$$\Delta u = \chi_S \left(f - \frac{\mathcal{M}(f)}{\mathcal{M}(\chi_S)} \right), \tag{12.4}$$

---

[72] In fact, in various papers, for example Zhou and Schölkopf [206], the graph p-Laplacian from (3.13) – which is the one derived from the graph p-Dirichlet energy – is not used, but rather the p-Laplacian derived by discretizing the continuum p-Laplacian; see footnote 22.

[73] For a brief overview of the connection between random walks and the graph Laplace equation, we refer to Van Gennip [188, Supplementary materials, section 2] and the references therein.

where f is as in (12.2). The choice $r = 0$ is made for the Laplacian Δ and mass functional $\mathcal{M}$. To select a unique solution, the constraint $\mathcal{M}(u) = 0$ is imposed, where this time $r = 1$ is chosen in $\mathcal{M}$.[74] As in the case of Laplace learning, to go from the real-valued function u to labels, a (mass-conserving) thresholding step is used. This is extended to multiple labels (see Section 11) and implemented using a multiclass variant of the mass-conserving fidelity-forced graph MBO scheme (version 2) from Section 8.3, which is named the Poisson MBO algorithm in [44]. Indeed, in the two-class case we see that the stationary solution to the diffusion step of this Poisson graph MBO scheme – namely to the mass-conserving fidelity-forced diffusion step of the mass-conserving fidelity-forced graph MBO scheme (version 2) – satisfies (12.4) with χ_S in the right-hand side replaced by μ with support equal to S.

Per [44, theorem 2.3], the equivalent variational formulation of (12.4) is[75]

$$u \in \operatorname*{argmin}_{v \in \mathcal{V}} \frac{1}{2} \|\nabla v\|_{\mathcal{E}}^2 - \left\langle \chi_S \left(f - \frac{\mathcal{M}(f)}{\mathcal{M}(\chi_S)} \right), v \right\rangle_{\mathcal{V}} \quad \text{s.t.} \quad \mathcal{M}(v) = 0.$$

For an interpretation of Poisson learning in terms of random walks, we refer to [44, theorem 2.1]. In appendix B of [190] we have a detailed look at solutions of (12.4).

In the recent work of Thorpe and Wang [184] a robust certification against adversarial attacks is proved for graph Laplace learning, that is, the classification result remains unchanged if the data points (assumed to be embedded in $\mathbb{R}^m$) are perturbed with some bounded perturbation. Work currently in preparation of Korolev *et al.* [122] studies Laplace learning in an infinite-dimensional setting.

13 Conclusions

Using the tools discribed in Section 3, discretized variants of differential equations and variational models can be formulated on graphs. We have focused mostly on the graph Ginzburg–Landau model and dynamics related to that model, such as those described by the graph Allen–Cahn equation, the graph MBO scheme, and graph mean curvature flow. In Section 12 we also had a look at the graph Laplace equation and graph Poisson equation.

A common theme that unites these various models and equations, besides being discretized versions of well-known continuum variational models and PDEs, is their application in machine learning and mathematical imaging.

---

[74] For a brief discussion of a redefined Poisson learning which uses a consistent r and which generalizes the Laplacian used to the two-parameter Laplacian $\Delta^{(s,t)}$ from (3.7), see Budd [34].

[75] To be consistent with [44], again we must choose $r = 0$, except in the constraint $\mathcal{M}(v) = 0$, where $r = 1$.

Besides containing extended versions of some of the sections from the current book, the companion volume, [190], also contains a full chapter about these applications in machine learning and imaging. It has another chapter dealing with the numerical implementation of these methods, a chapter about the connections between the graph Allen–Cahn equation, the graph MBO scheme, and graph mean curvature flow, and a chapter about discrete-to-continuum limits of graph-based models. Furthermore, it contains a, necessarily relatively brief, overview of the continuum models from which the graph-based models are derived, and a discussion of connections with other fields and open questions.

If this work is part of a snapshot of the current state of this very active mathematical field, then its companion is meant to be a fuller and broader overview. While both works contain a literature overview that can suggest further directions to explore for the interested reader, the companion volume contains a significantly more extensive bibliography to explore.

References

[1] Abiad, Aida, Mulas, Raffaella, and Zhang, Dong. 2021. Coloring the normalized Laplacian for oriented hypergraphs. *Linear Algebra and Its Applications*, **629**, 192–207.

[2] Açıkmeşe, Behçet. 2015. *Spectrum of Laplacians for Graphs with Self-Loops.* arXiv:1505.08133 [math.OC].

[3] Albin, Nathan, Brunner, Megan, Perez, Roberto, Poggi-Corradini, Pietro, and Wiens, Natalie. 2015. Modulus on graphs as a generalization of standard graph theoretic quantities. *Conformal Geometry and Dynamics of the American Mathematical Society*, **19**(13), 298–317.

[4] Alicandro, Roberto, Ansini, Nadia, Braides, Andrea, Piatnitski, Andrey, and Tribuzio, Antonio. 2023. *A Variational Theory of Convolution-Type Functionals.* SpringerBriefs on PDEs and Data Science. Singapore: Springer.

[5] Allen, Samuel M., and Cahn, John W. 1979. A microscopic theory for antiphase boundary motion and its application to antiphase domain coarsening. *Acta Metallurgica*, **27**(6), 1085–1095.

[6] Almgren, Fred, Taylor, Jean E., and Wang, Lihe. 1993. Curvature-driven flows: a variational approach. *SIAM Journal on Control and Optimization*, **31**(2), 387–438.

[7] Alon, Noga. 1986. Eigenvalues and expanders. *Combinatorica*, **6**(2), 83–96. DOI: https://doi.org/10.1007/BF02579166.

[8] Alon, Noga, and Milman, Vitali D. 1985. λ_1, isoperimetric inequalities for graphs, and superconcentrators. *The Journal of Combinatorial Theory, Series B*, **38**(1), 73–88.

[9] Andreu, Fuensanta, Ballester, Coloma, Caselles, Vicent, and Mazón, José M. 2001. Minimizing total variation flow. *Differential and Integral Equations*, **14**(3), 321–360.

[10] Arora, Sanjeev, Hazan, Elad, and Kale, Satyen. 2010. $O(\sqrt{\log n})$ approximation to SPARSEST CUT in $\tilde{O}(n^2)$ time. *SIAM Journal on Computing*, **39**(5), 1748–1771.

[11] Aviles-Rivero, Angelica I., Runkel, Christina, Papadakis, Nicolas, Kourtzi, Zoe, and Schönlieb, Carola-Bibiane. 2022. Multi-modal hypergraph diffusion network with dual prior for Alzheimer classification. Pages 717–727 of Wang, Linwei, Dou, Qi, Fletcher, P. Thomas, Speidel, Stefanie, and Li, Shuo (eds.), *Medical Image Computing and Computer Assisted Intervention: MICCAI 2022.* Cham: Springer Nature.

[12] Avrachenkov, Konstantin, Chebotarev, Pavel, and Rubanov, Dmytro. 2019. Similarities on graphs: kernels versus proximity measures. *European Journal of Combinatorics*, **80**, 47–56.

[13] Bae, Egil, and Merkurjev, Ekaterina. 2017. Convex variational methods on graphs for multiclass segmentation of high-dimensional data and point clouds. *Journal of Mathematical Imaging and Vision*, **58**, 468–493.

[14] Bagirov, Adil, Karmitsa, Napsu, and Mäkelä, Marko M. 2014. *Introduction to Nonsmooth Optimization*. Cham: Springer.

[15] Barabási, Albert-László. 2016. *Network Science*. Cambridge: Cambridge University Press.

[16] Barles, Guy, and Georgelin, Christine. 1995. A simple proof of convergence for an approximation scheme for computing motions by mean curvature. *SIAM Journal on Numerical Analysis*, **32**(2), 484–500.

[17] Bauer, Frank. 2012. Normalized graph Laplacians for directed graphs. *Linear Algebra and Its Applications*, **436**(11), 4193–4222.

[18] Belongie, Serge, Fowlkes, Charless, Chung, Fan, and Malik, Jitendra. 2002. Spectral partitioning with indefinite kernels using the Nyström extension. Pages 531–542 of Heyden, Anders, Sparr, Gunnar, Nielsen, Mads, and Johansen, Peter (eds.), *European Conference on Computer Vision*. Berlin: Springer. https://link.springer.com/book/10 .1007/3-540-47969-4

[19] Bendito, Enrique, Carmona, Ángeles, and Encinas, Andrés M. 2003. Solving Dirichlet and Poisson problems on graphs by means of equilibrium measures. *European Journal of Combinatorics*, **24**(4), 365–375.

[20] Bertozzi, Andrea L. 2018. Graphical models in machine learning, networks, and uncertainty quantification. Pages 3853–3880 of Sirakov, Boyan, Ney de Souza, Paulo, and Viana, Marcelo (eds.), *Proceedings of the International Congress of Mathematicians*, vol. 3. Singapore: World Scientific.

[21] Bertozzi, Andrea L., and Flenner, Arjuna. 2012. Diffuse interface models on graphs for classification of high dimensional data. *Multiscale Modeling & Simulation*, **10**(3), 1090–1118.

[22] Bertozzi, Andrea L., and Flenner, Arjuna. 2016. Diffuse interface models on graphs for classification of high dimensional data. *SIAM Review*, **58**(2), 293–328.

[23] Bertozzi, Andrea L., and Merkurjev, Ekaterina. 2019. Graph-based optimization approaches for machine learning, uncertainty quantification and networks. Pages 503–531 of Kimmel, Ron, and Tai, Xue-Cheng (eds.), *Processing, Analyzing and Learning of Images, Shapes, and*

Forms: Part 2. Handbook of Numerical Analysis, vol. 20. Amsterdam: Elsevier.

[24] Bühler, Thomas, and Hein, Matthias. 2009. Spectral clustering based on the graph *p*-Laplacian. Pages 81–88 of *Proceedings of the 26th Annual International Conference on Machine Learning*. New York, NY: Association for Computing Machinery.

[25] Bonaccorsi, Stefano, Cottini, Francesca, and Mugnolo, Delio. 2021. Random Evolution equations: Well-posedness, asymptotics, and applications to graphs. *Applied Mathematics and Optimization*, **84**, 2849–2887.

[26] Bosch, Jessica, Klamt, Steffen, and Stoll, Martin. 2018. Generalizing diffuse interface methods on graphs: nonsmooth potentials and hypergraphs. *SIAM Journal on Applied Mathematics*, **7**(3), 1350–1377.

[27] Boyd, Zachary M., Bae, Egil, Tai, Xue-Cheng, and Bertozzi, Andrea L. 2018. Simplified energy landscape for modularity using total variation. *SIAM Journal on Applied Mathematics*, **78**(5), 2439–2464.

[28] Braides, Andrea. 2002. Γ-*Convergence for Beginners*. Oxford Lecture Series in Mathematics and Its Applications, vol. 22. Oxford: Oxford University Press.

[29] Braides, Andrea, Gelli, Maria Stella, and Novaga, Matteo. 2010. Motion and pinning of discrete interfaces. *Archive for Rational Mechanics and Analysis*, **195**(2), 469–498.

[30] Brakke, Kenneth A. 1978. *The Motion of a Surface by Its Mean Curvature*. Mathematical Notes, vol. 20. Princeton, NJ: Princeton University Press.

[31] Bresson, Xavier, Hu, Huiyi, Laurent, Thomas, Szlam, Arthur, and von Brecht, James. 2018. An incremental reseeding strategy for clustering. Pages 203–219 of Tai, Xue-Cheng, Bae, Egil, and Lysaker, Marius (eds.), *International Conference on Imaging, Vision and Learning based on Optimization and PDEs – IVLOPDE 2016: Imaging, Vision and Learning Based on Optimization and PDEs*. Mathematics and Visualization. Cham: Springer International.

[32] Bronsard, Lia, and Kohn, Robert V. 1991. Motion by mean curvature as the singular limit of Ginzburg–Landau dynamics. *Journal of Differential Equations*, **90**(2), 211–237.

[33] Budd, Jeremy. 2022. Theory and Applications of PDE Methods in Graph-Based Learning. PhD thesis, Delft University of Technology.

[34] Budd, Jeremy. 2023. *Graph-Based Learning for Image Processing*. https://jeremybudd.com/. Online lecture notes; accessed 7 August 2023.

[35] Budd, Jeremy, and van Gennip, Yves. 2020. Graph Merriman–Bence–Osher as a semidiscrete implicit Euler scheme for graph Allen–Cahn flow. *SIAM Journal on Mathematical Analysis*, **52**(5), 4101–4139.

[36] Budd, Jeremy, and van Gennip, Yves. 2022. Mass-conserving diffusion-based dynamics on graphs. *European Journal of Applied Mathematics*, **33**(3), 423–471.

[37] Budd, Jeremy, van Gennip, Yves, and Latz, Jonas. 2021. Classification and image processing with a semi-discrete scheme for fidelity forced Allen–Cahn on graphs. *GAMM Mitteilungen Special Issue: Scientific Machine Learning – Part I*, **44**, 1–43.

[38] Böhle, Tobias, Kuehn, Christian, Mulas, Raffaella, and Jost, Jürgen. 2022. Coupled hypergraph maps and chaotic cluster synchronization. *Europhysics Letters*, **136**(4), 40005.

[39] Caffarelli, Luis A., and Souganidis, Panagiotis E. 2010. Convergence of nonlocal threshold dynamics approximations to front propagation. *Archive for Rational Mechanics and Analysis*, **195**(1), 1–23.

[40] Cahn, John W., and Hilliard, John E. 1958. Free energy of a nonuniform system. I. Interfacial free energy. *The Journal of Chemical Physics*, **28**(2), 258–267.

[41] Calatroni, Luca, van Gennip, Yves, Schönlieb, Carola-Bibiane, Rowland, Hannah M., and Flenner, Arjuna. 2017. Graph clustering, variational image segmentation methods and Hough transform scale detection for object measurement in images. *Journal of Mathematical Imaging and Vision*, **57**, 269–291.

[42] Calder, Jeff, and Ettehad, Mahmood. 2022. Hamilton–Jacobi equations on graphs with applications to semi-supervised learning and data depth. *Journal of Machine Learning Research*, **23**(318), 1–62.

[43] Calder, Jeff, and Slepčev, Dejan. 2020. Properly-weighted graph Laplacian for semisupervised learning. *Applied Mathematics and Optimization*, **82**, 1111–1159.

[44] Calder, Jeff, Cook, Brendan, Thorpe, Matthew, and Slepčev, Dejan. 2020. Poisson learning: graph based semi-supervised learning at very low label rates. Pages 1306–1316 of Daumé III, Hal, and Singh, Aarti (eds.), *Proceedings of the 37th International Conference on Machine Learning*. Proceedings of Machine Learning Research, vol. 119.

[45] Calder, Jeff, García Trillos, Nicolás, and Lewicka, Marta. 2022. Lipschitz regularity of graph Laplacians on random data clouds. *SIAM Journal on Mathematical Analysis*, **54**(1), 1169–1222.

[46] Chan, Tony F., and Shen, Jianhong (Jackie). 2005. *Image Processing and Analysis*. Philadelphia, PA: Society for Industrial and Applied Mathematics.

[47] Chan, Tony F., and Vese, Luminita A. 2001. Active contours without edges. *IEEE Transactions on Image Processing*, **10**(2), 266–277.

[48] Chebotarev, Pavel. 2013. Studying new classes of graph metrics. Pages 207–214 of Nielsen, Frank, and Barbaresco, Frédéric (eds.), *Geometric Science of Information: Proceedings of the First International Conference GSI 2013*. Berlin: Springer.

[49] Cheeger, Jeff. 1970. A lower bound for the smallest eigenvalue of the Laplacian. Pages 195–199 Gunning, Robert C. (ed.), *Problems in analysis (Papers dedicated to Salomon Bochner, 1969)*. Princeton, NJ: Princeton University Press.

[50] Chen, Yun Gang, Giga, Yoshikazu, and Goto, Shun'ichi. 1991. Uniqueness and existence of viscosity solutions of generalized mean curvature flow equations. *Journal of Differential Geometry*, **33**(3), 749–786.

[51] Chong, Yanwen, Ding, Yun, Yan, Qing, and Pan, Shaoming. 2020. Graph-based semi-supervised learning: a review. *Neurocomputing*, **408**, 216–230.

[52] Chung, Fan. 2005. Laplacians and the Cheeger inequality for directed graphs. *Annals of Combinatorics*, **9**, 1–19.

[53] Chung, Fan, and Yau, Shing-Tung. 2000. Discrete Green's Functions. *Journal of Combinatorial Theory, Series A*, **91**(1), 191–214.

[54] Chung, Fan, and Yau, Shing-Tung. 2007. *Discrete Green's functions*. https://mathweb.ucsd.edu/~fan/wp/green.pdf. Online version of [53] with additional revisions, file dated 4 December 2007; accessed 29 August 2022.

[55] Chung, Fan R. K. 1997. *Spectral Graph Theory*. CBMS Regional Conference Series in Mathematics, vol. 92. Providence, RI: American Mathematical Society.

[56] Clarenz, Ulrich, Haußer, Frank, Rumpf, Martin, Voigt, Axel, and Weikard, Ulrich. 2005. On level set formulations for anisotropic mean curvature flow and surface diffusion. Pages 227–237 of Voigt, Axel (ed.), *Multiscale Modeling in Epitaxial Growth*. International Series of Numerical Mathematics, vol. 149. Basel: Birkhäuser.

[57] Corless, Robert M., Gonnet, Gaston H., Hare, David E. G., Jeffrey, David J., and Knuth, Donald E. 1996. On the Lambert W function. *Advances in Computational Mathematics*, **5**, 329–359.

[58] Coulhon, Thierry, and Koskela, Pekka. 2004. Geometric interpretations of L^p-Poincaré inequalities on graphs with polynomial volume growth. *Milan Journal of Mathematics*, **72**, 209–248.

[59] Crook, Oliver M., Hurst, Tim, Schönlieb, Carola-Bibiane, Thorpe, Matthew, and Zygalakis, Konstantinos C. 2019. *PDE-Inspired Algorithms for Semi-Supervised Learning on Point Clouds*. arxiv.org/abs/1909.10221v1 [math.NA].

[60] Cucuringu, Mihai, Pizzoferrato, Andrea, and van Gennip, Yves. 2021. An MBO scheme for clustering and semi-supervised clustering of signed networks. *Communications in Mathematical Sciences*, **19**(1), 73–109.

[61] Dacorogna, Bernard, Gangbo, Wilfrid, and Subía, Nelson. 1992. Sur une généralisation de l'inégalité de Wirtinger. *Annales de l'Institut Henri Poincaré / Analyse non linéaire*, **9**(1), 29–50.

[62] Dal Maso, Gianni. 1993. *An Introduction to Γ-Convergence*. first ed. Progress in Nonlinear Differential Equations and Their Applications, vol. 8. Boston, MA: Birkhäuser.

[63] Desquesnes, Xavier, Elmoataz, Abderrahim, and Lézoray, Olivier. 2012. Generalized fronts propagation on weighted graphs. Pages 371–381 of *Proceedings of ALGORITMY: 19th Conference on Scientific Computing, 2012, Slovakia*. Bratislava: Comenius University, Department of Applied Mathematics and Statistics. www.iam.fmph.uniba.sk/amuc/ojs/index.php/algoritmy/issue/view/18

[64] Ding, Chris H. Q., He, Xiaofeng, Zha, Hongyuan, Gu, Ming, and Simon, Horst D. 2001. A min-max cut algorithm for graph partitioning and data clustering. Pages 107–114 of Cercone, Nick, Lin, Tsau Young, and Wu, Xindong (eds.), *Proceedings 2001 IEEE International Conference on Data Mining*. Washington, DC: IEEE Computer Society. https://ieeexplore.ieee.org/xpl/conhome/7762/proceeding.

[65] Ding, Xiucai, and Wu, Hau-Tieng. 2022. Impact of signal-to-noise ratio and bandwidth on graph Laplacian spectrum from high-dimensional noisy point cloud. *IEEE Transactions on Information Theory*, **69**(3), 1899–1931.

[66] Dym, Harry, and McKean, Henry Pratt. 1985. *Fourier Series and Integrals*. Elsevier Academic Press.

[67] Ekeland, Ivar, and Temam, Roger. 1976. *Convex Analysis and Variational Problems*. Amsterdam: North-Holland. Translated from the French, Studies in Mathematics and Its Applications, Vol. 1.

[68] El Bouchairi, Imad. 2021. Partial differential equations on graphs: continuum limits on sparse graphs and applications. PhD thesis, University of Caen Normandy.

[69] El Bouchairi, Imad, Elmoataz, Abderrahim, and Fadili, Jalal M. 2023. Nonlocal perimeters and curvature flows on graphs with applications in image processing and high-dimensional data classification. *SIAM Journal on Imaging Sciences*, **16**(1), 368–392.

[70] El Chakik, Abdallah, Elmoataz, Abderrahim, and Desquesnes, Xavier. 2014. Mean curvature flow on graphs for image and manifold restoration and enhancement. *Signal Processing*, **105**, 449–463.

[71] Elek, Gábor, and Szegedy, Balázs. 2012. A measure-theoretic approach to the theory of dense hypergraphs. *Advances in Mathematics*, **231**(3), 1731–1772.

[72] Elmoataz, Abderrahim, Desquesnes, Xavier, and Lézoray, Olivier. 2012. Non-local morphological PDEs and p-Laplacian equation on graphs with applications in image processing and machine learning. *IEEE Journal of Selected Topics in Signal Processing*, **6**(7), 764–779.

[73] Elmoataz, Abderrahim, Desquesnes, Xavier, Lakhdari, Zakaria, and Lézoray, Olivier. 2014. Nonlocal infinity Laplacian equation on graphs with applications in image processing and machine learning. *Mathematics and Computers in Simulation*, **102**, 153–163. 4th International Conference on Approximation Methods and Numerical Modeling in Environment and Natural Resources: PART II.

[74] Elmoataz, Abderrahim, Desquesnes, Xavier, and Toutain, Matthieu. 2017. On the game p-Laplacian on weighted graphs with applications in image processing and data clustering. *European Journal of Applied Mathematics*, **28**(6), 922–948.

[75] Elmoataz, Abderrahim, Lézoray, Olivier, and Bougleux, Sébastien. 2008. Nonlocal discrete p-Laplacian driven image and manifold processing. *Comptes Rendus Mecanique*, **336**(5), 428–433.

[76] Elmoataz, Abderrahim, Toutain, Matthieu, and Tenbrinck, Daniel. 2015. On the p-Laplacian and ∞-Laplacian on graphs with applications in image and data processing. *SIAM Journal on Imaging Sciences*, **8**(4), 2412–2451.

[77] Esedoğlu, Selim, and Otto, Felix. 2015. Threshold dynamics for networks with arbitrary surface tensions. *Communications on Pure and Applied Mathematics*, **68**(5), 808–864.

[78] Estrada, Ernesto, and Knight, Philip Anthony. 2015. *A First Course in Network Theory*. Oxford: Oxford University Press.

[79] Estrada, Ernesto, and Mugnolo, Delio. 2022. Hubs-biased resistance distances on graphs and networks. *Journal of Mathematical Analysis and Applications*, **507**(1), 125728.

[80] Evans, Lawrence C. 1993. Convergence of an algorithm for mean curvature motion. *Indiana University Mathematics Journal*, **42**(2), 533–557.

[81] Evans, Lawrence C. 2010. *Partial Differential Equations*. Second ed. Graduate Studies in Mathematics, vol. 19. Providence, RI: American Mathematical Society.

[82] Evans, Lawrence C., and Spruck, Joel. 1991. Motion of level sets by mean curvature. I. *Journal of Differential Geometry*, **33**(3), 635–681.

[83] Evans, Lawrence C., and Spruck, Joel. 1992a. Motion of level sets by mean curvature. II. *Transactions of the American Mathematical Society*, **330**(1), 321–332.

[84] Evans, Lawrence C., and Spruck, Joel. 1992b. Motion of level sets by mean curvature. III. *The Journal of Geometric Analysis*, **2**(2), 121–150.

[85] Evans, Lawrence C., and Spruck, Joel. 1995. Motion of level sets by mean curvature. IV. *The Journal of Geometric Analysis*, **5**(1), 77–114.

[86] Fanuel, Michaël, Alaíz, Carlos M., Fernández, Ángela, and Suykens, Johan A. K. 2018. Magnetic eigenmaps for the visualization of directed networks. *Applied and Computational Harmonic Analysis*, **44**(1), 189–199.

[87] Fanuel, Michaël, Alaíz, Carlos M., and Suykens, Johan A. K. 2017. Magnetic eigenmaps for community detection in directed networks. *Physical Review E*, **95**(Feb), 022302.

[88] Fazeny, Ariane. 2023. p-Laplacian Operators on Hypergraphs. arXiv:2304.06468 [math.OC]. M.Sc. thesis.

[89] Fazeny, Ariane, Tenbrinck, Daniel, and Burger, Martin. 2023. Hypergraph p-Laplacians, scale spaces, and information flow in networks. Pages 677–690 of Calatroni, Luca, Donatelli, Marco, Morigi, Serena, Prato, Marco, and Santacesaria, Matteo (eds.), *Scale Space and Variational Methods in Computer Vision*. Lecture Notes in Computer Science (LNCS), vol. 14009. Cham: Springer International.

[90] Flores, Mauricio, Calder, Jeff, and Lerman, Gilad. 2022. Analysis and algorithms for ℓ_p-based semi-supervised learning on graphs. *Applied and Computational Harmonic Analysis*, **60**, 77–122.

[91] Forman, Robin. 2003. Bochner's method for cell complexes and combinatorial Ricci curvature. *Discrete & Computational Geometry*, **29**(3), 323–374.

[92] Galuppi, Francesco, Mulas, Raffaella, and Venturello, Lorenzo. 2023. Spectral theory of weighted hypergraphs via tensors. *Linear Multilinear Algebra*, **71**(3), 317–347.

[93] Garcia-Cardona, Cristina, Flenner, Arjuna, and Percus, Allon G. 2013. Multiclass diffuse interface models for semi-supervised learning on graphs. Pages 78–86 of Fred, Ana, and De Marsico, Maria (eds.), *Proceedings of the 2nd International Conference on Pattern Recognition Applications and Methods (ICPRAM 2013)*. Springer Nature. https://link.springer.com/book/10.1007/978-3-319-12610-4.

[94] Garcia-Cardona, Cristina, Flenner, Arjuna, and Percus, Allon G. 2015. Multiclass semi-supervised learning on graphs using Ginzburg–Landau functional minimization. Pages 119–135 of Fred, Ana, and De Marsico, Maria (eds.), *Pattern Recognition Applications and Methods*. Advances in Intelligent Systems and Computing (AISC), vol. 318. Cham: Springer International.

[95] Garcia-Cardona, Cristina, Merkurjev, Ekaterina, Bertozzi, Andrea L., Flenner, Arjuna, and Percus, Allon G. 2014. Multiclass data segmentation using diffuse interface methods on graphs. *IEEE Transactions on Pattern Analysis and Machine Intelligence*, **36**(8), 1600–1613.

[96] García Trillos, Nicolás, and Weber, Melanie. 2023. *Continuum Limits of Ollivier's Ricci Curvature on data clouds: pointwise consistency and global lower bounds*. arxiv.org/abs/2307.02378v1 [math.DG].

[97] García Trillos, Nicolás, Sanz-Alonso, Daniel, and Yang, Ruiyi. 2019. Local regularization of noisy point clouds: improved global geometric estimates and data analysis. *Journal of Machine Learning Research*, **20**(136), 1–37.

[98] Ghosh, Rumi, and Lerman, Kristina. 2014. Rethinking centrality: the role of dynamical processes in social network analysis. *Discrete & Continuous Dynamical Systems: Series B*, **19**(5), 1355–1372.

[99] Goemans, Michel X., and Williamson, David P. 1995. Improved approximation algorithms for maximum cut and satisfiability problems using semidefinite programming. *Journal of the ACM (JACM)*, **42**(6), 1115–1145.

[100] Gong, Xue, Higham, Desmond J., and Zygalakis, Konstantinos. 2021. Directed network Laplacians and random graph models. *Royal Society Open Science*, **8**(211144).

[101] Grady, Leo J., and Polimeni, Jonathan R. 2010. *Discrete Calculus: Applied Analysis on Graphs for Computational Science*. London: Springer.

[102] Hagen, Lars, and Kahng, Andrew B. 1992. New spectral methods for ratio cut partitioning and clustering. *IEEE Transactions on Computer-Aided Design of Integrated Circuits and Systems*, **11**(9), 1074–1085.

[103] Hale, Jack K. 2009. *Ordinary Differential Equations*. Second ed. Mineola, NY: Dover.

[104] Hein, Matthias, Audibert, Jean-Yves, and von Luxburg, Ulrike. 2007. Graph Laplacians and their convergence on random neighborhood graphs. *Journal of Machine Learning Research*, **8**, 1325–1368.

[105] Hoffmann, Franca, Hosseini, Bamdad, Oberai, Assad A., and Stuart, Andrew M. 2022. Spectral analysis of weighted Laplacians arising in data clustering. *Applied and Computational Harmonic Analysis*, **56**, 189–249.

[106] Hu, Huiyi, Sunu, Justin, and Bertozzi, Andrea L. 2015. Multi-class graph Mumford–Shah model for plume detection using the MBO scheme. Pages 209–222 of Tai, Xue-Cheng, Bae, Egil, Chan, Tony F., and Lysaker, Marius (eds.), *Energy Minimization Methods in Computer Vision and Pattern Recognition*. Cham: Springer International.

[107] Iacono, Roberto, and Boyd, John P. 2017. New approximations to the principal real-valued branch of the Lambert W-function. *Advances in Computational Mathematics*, **43**(6), 1403–1436.

[108] Ikeda, Masahiro, and Uchida, Shun. 2023. Nonlinear evolution equation associated with hypergraph Laplacian. *Mathematical Methods in the Applied Sciences*, **46**(8), 9463–9476.

[109] Izenman, Alan Julian. 2023. *Network Models for Data Science: Theory, Algorithms, and Applications*. Cambridge: Cambridge University Press.

[110] Jacobs, Matt, Merkurjev, Ekaterina, and Esedoğlu, Selim. 2018. Auction dynamics: a volume constrained MBO scheme. *Journal of Computational Physics*, **354**, 288–310.

[111] Jost, Jürgen, and Münch, Florentin. 2021. *Characterizations of Forman Curvature*. arxiv.org/abs/2110.04554v1 [math.DG].

[112] Jost, Jürgen, and Mulas, Raffaella. 2019. Hypergraph Laplace operators for chemical reaction networks. *Advances in Mathematics*, **351**, 870–896.

[113] Jost, Jürgen, Mulas, Raffaella, and Zhang, Dong. 2022. p-Laplace operators for oriented hypergraphs. *Vietnam Journal of Mathematics*, **50**(2), 323–358.

[114] Jost, Jürgen, Mulas, Raffaella, and Torres, Leo. 2023. Spectral theory of the non-backtracking Laplacian for graphs. *Discrete Mathematics*, **346**(10), 113536.

[115] Karoui, Noureddine El, and Wu, Hau-Tieng. 2016. Graph connection Laplacian methods can be made robust to noise. *The Annals of Statistics*, **44**(1), 346–372.

[116] Keetch, Blaine. 2020. Applying partial differential equations on networks to approximate the Max-Cut and Max-K-Cut problems. PhD thesis, University of Nottingham.

[117] Keetch, Blaine, and van Gennip, Yves. 2019. A Max-Cut approximation using a graph based MBO scheme. *Discrete and Continuous Dynamical Systems: Series B*, **24**(11), 6091–6139.

[118] Kennedy, James B., Kurasov, Pavel, Léna, Corentin, and Mugnolo, Delio. 2021. A theory of spectral partitions of metric graphs. *Calculus of Variations and Partial Differential Equations*, **60**(61).

[119] Klus, Stefan, and Djurdjevac Conrad, Nataša. 2023. Koopman-based spectral clustering of directed and time-evolving graphs. *Journal of Nonlinear Science*, **33**(1), Paper No. 8, 22.

[120] Knight, Philip A., and Ruiz, Daniel. 2013. A fast algorithm for matrix balancing. *IMA Journal of Numerical Analysis*, **33**(3), 1029–1047.

[121] Knill, Oliver, and Rak, Annie. 2016. Differential equations on graphs. https://people.math.harvard.edu/~knill//pde/pde.pdf. HCRP Summer 2016 program project notes.

[122] Korolev, Yury, Kuger, Lorenz, and Thorpe, Matthew. Laplace Learning for Feature Vectors in Hilbert Spaces. In preparation.

[123] Kyng, Rasmus, Rao, Anup, Sachdeva, Sushant, and Spielman, Daniel A. 2015. Algorithms for Lipschitz learning on graphs. Pages 1190–1223 of Grünwald, Peter, Hazan, Elad, and Kale, Satyen (eds.), *Proceedings of the 28th Conference on Learning Theory*. Proceedings of Machine Learning Research, vol. 40. Paris: Proceedings of Machine Learning Research.

[124] Laux, Tim, and Lelmi, Jona. 2021. Large data limit of the MBO scheme for data clustering: Γ-convergence of the thresholding energies. arXiv:2112.06737 [math.AP].

[125] Laux, Tim, and Lelmi, Jona. 2022. De Giorgi's inequality for the thresholding scheme with arbitrary mobilities and surface tensions. *Calculus of Variations and Partial Differential Equations*, **61**(35).

[126] Laux, Tim, and Yip, Nung Kwan. 2019. Analysis of diffusion generated motion for mean curvature flow in codimension two: a gradient-flow

approach. *Archive for Rational Mechanics and Analysis*, **232**, 1113–1163.

[127] le Gorrec, Luce, Mouysset, Sandrine, Duff, Iain S., Knight, Philip Anthony, and Ruiz, Daniel. 2020. Uncovering hidden block structure for clustering. Pages 140–155 of Brefeld, Ulf, Fromont, Elisa, Hotho, Andreas, Knobbe, Arno, Maathuis, Marloes, and Robardet, Céline (eds.), *Machine Learning and Knowledge Discovery in Databases*. Lecture Notes in Computer Science (LNAI), vol. 11906. Cham: Springer International.

[128] Lee, James R., Oveis Gharan, Shayan, and Trevisan, Luca. 2014. Multiway spectral partitioning and higher-order Cheeger inequalities. *Journal of the ACM*, **61**(6).

[129] Levi, Matteo, Santagati, Federico, Tabacco, Anita, and Vallarino, Maria. 2023. Poincaré inequalities on graphs. *Analysis Mathematica*, **49**(2), 529–544.

[130] Lovász, László. 2009. *Geometric Representations of Graphs*. https://web.cs.elte.hu/ lovasz/geomrep.pdf. Online notes; accessed 4 August 2022.

[131] Lozes, François, Elmoataz, Abderrahim, and Lézoray, Olivier. 2012. Nonlocal processing of 3D colored point clouds. Pages 1968–1971 of *Proceedings of the 21st International Conference on Pattern Recognition (ICPR2012)*. New York, NY: IEEE. https://ieeexplore.ieee.org/xpl/conhome/6425799/proceeding.

[132] Luckhaus, Stephan, and Sturzenhecker, Thomas. 1995. Implicit time discretization for the mean curvature flow equation. *Calculus of Variations and Partial Differential Equations*, **3**(2), 253–271.

[133] Macgregor, Peter. 2022. *On Learning the Structure of Clusters in Graphs*. arxiv.org/abs/2212.14345 [cs.DS]. PhD thesis, University of Edinburgh.

[134] Macgregor, Peter, and Sun, He. 2021a. Finding bipartite components in hypergraphs. Pages 7912–7923 of Ranzato, Marc'Aurelio, Beygelzimer, Alina, Dauphin, Yann N., Liang, Percy S., and Wortman Vaughan, Jennifer (eds.), *Advances in Neural Information Processing Systems*, vol. 34. New York, NY: Curran Associates.

[135] Macgregor, Peter, and Sun, He. 2021b. Local algorithms for finding densely connected clusters. Pages 7268–7278 of Meila, Marina, and Zhang, Tong (eds.), *Proceedings of the 38th International Conference on Machine Learning*. Proceedings of Machine Learning Research, vol. 139.

[136] Macgregor, Peter, and Sun, He. 2022. A tighter analysis of spectral clustering, and beyond. Pages 14717–14742 of Chaudhuri, Kamalika, Jegelka, Stefanie, Song, Le, Szepesvari, Csaba, Niu, Gang, and Sabato, Sivan (eds.), *Proceedings of the 39th International Conference on Machine Learning*. Proceedings of Machine Learning Research, vol. 162.

[137] MacKay, Robert S., Johnson, Samuel, and Sansom, Brandon 2020. How directed is a directed network? *Royal Society Open Science*, 7(201138).

[138] Manfredi, Juan J., Oberman, Adam M., and Sviridov, Alexander P. 2015. Nonlinear elliptic partial differential equations and p-harmonic functions on graphs. *Differential Integral Equations*, **28**(1–2), 79–102.

[139] Mazón, José M., Solera, Marcos, and Toledo, Julián. 2020a. The heat flow on metric random walk spaces. *Journal of Mathematical Analysis and Applications*, **483**(2), 123645.

[140] Mazón, José M., Solera, Marcos, and Toledo, Julián. 2020b. The total variation flow in metric random walk spaces. *Calculus of Variations and Partial Differential Equations*, **59**(29), 1–64.

[141] Merkurjev, Ekaterina, Bertozzi, Andrea, Yan, Xiaoran, and Lerman, Kristina. 2017. Modified Cheeger and ratio cut methods using the Ginzburg–Landau functional for classification of high-dimensional data. *Inverse Problems*, **33**, 074003.

[142] Merkurjev, Ekaterina, Bertozzi, Andrea L., and Chung, Fan. 2018. A semi-supervised heat kernel pagerank MBO algorithm for data classification. *Communications in Mathematical Sciences*, **16**(5), 1241–1264.

[143] Merkurjev, Ekaterina, Garcia-Cardona, Cristina, Bertozzi, Andrea L., Flenner, Arjuna, and Percus, Allon G. 2014. Diffuse interface methods for multiclass segmentation of high-dimensional data. *Applied Mathematics Letters*, **33**, 29–34.

[144] Merkurjev, Ekaterina, Kostic, Tijana, and Bertozzi, Andrea L. 2013. An MBO scheme on graphs for segmentation and image processing. *SIAM Journal on Imaging Sciences*, **6**(4), 1903–1930.

[145] Merkurjev, Ekaterina, Nguyen, Duc Duy, and Wei, Guo-Wei. 2022. Multiscale laplacian learning. *Applied Intelligence*, **53**, 15727–15746.

[146] Merriman, Barry, Bence, James K., and Osher, Stanley J. 1992. *Diffusion Generated Motion by Mean Curvature*. UCLA Department of Mathematics CAM report 92-18. https://ww3.math.ucla.edu/cam-reports-1986-2000/

[147] Merriman, Barry, Bence, James K., and Osher, Stanley J. 1993. Diffusion generated motion by mean curvature. *AMS Selected Letters, Crystal Grower's Workshop*, 73–83.

[148] Miller, Kevin, Mauro, John, Setiadi, Jason, Baca, Xoaquin, Shi, Zhan, Calder, Jeff, and Bertozzi, Andrea L. 2022. Graph-based active learning for semi-supervised classification of SAR data. Page 120950C of Zelnio, Edmund, and Garber, Frederick D. (eds.), *Algorithms for Synthetic Aperture Radar Imagery XXIX*, vol. 12095. SPIE.

[149] Misiats, Oleksandr, and Yip, Nung Kwan. 2016. Convergence of space-time discrete threshold dynamics to anisotropic motion by mean curvature. *Discrete and Continuous Dynamical Systems*, **36**(11), 6379–6411. https://www.aimsciences.org/article/doi/10.3934/dcds.2016076.

[150] Moreau, Luc. 2004. Stability of continuous-time distributed consensus algorithms. Pages 3998–4003 of *43rd IEEE Conference on Decision and Control*, vol. 4. DOI: https://doi.org10.1109/CDC.2004.1429377.

[151] Mucha, Peter J., Richardson, Thomas, Macon, Kevin, Porter, Mason A., and Onnela, Jukka-Pekka. 2010. Community structure in time-dependent, multiscale, and multiplex networks. *Science*, **328**(5980), 876–878.

[152] Münch, Florentin, and Wojciechowski, Radosław K. 2019. Ollivier Ricci curvature for general graph Laplacians: heat equation, Laplacian comparison, non-explosion and diameter bounds. *Advances in Mathematics*, **356**, 106759.

[153] Mugnolo, Delio. 2014. *Semigroup Methods for Evolution Equations on Networks*. Cham: Springer International.

[154] Mulas, Raffaella. 2021. A Cheeger cut for uniform hypergraphs. *Graphs and Combinatorics*, **37**(6), 2265–2286.

[155] Mulas, Raffaella, Horak, Danijela, and Jost, Jürgen. 2022a. *Graphs, simplicial complexes and hypergraphs: spectral theory and topology*. Pages 1–58 of Battiston, Federico, and Petri, Giovanni (eds.), *Higher-Order Systems*. Understanding Complex Systems. Cham: Springer International **36**(11).

[156] Mulas, Raffaella, Kuehn, Christian, Böhle, Tobias, and Jost, Jürgen. 2022b. Random walks and Laplacians on hypergraphs: when do they match? *Discrete Applied Mathematics*, **317**, 26–41.

[157] Mulas, Raffaella, and Zhang, Dong. 2021. Spectral theory of Laplace operators on oriented hypergraphs. *Discrete Mathematics*, **344**(6), 112372.

[158] Mulas, Raffaella, Zhang , Dong, and Zucal, Giulio. 2024. There is no going back: properties of the non-backtracking Laplacian. Linear Algebra and its Applications, **680**, 341–370. https://doi.org/10.1016/j.laa .2023.10.014.

[159] Mumford, David, and Shah, Jayant. 1989. Optimal approximations by piecewise smooth functions and associated variational problems. *Communications on Pure and Applied Mathematics*, **42**, 577–685. DOI: https://doi.org/10.1002/cpa.3160420503.

[160] Neuberger, John M. 2006. Nonlinear elliptic partial difference equations on graphs. *Experimental Mathematics*, **15**(1), 91–107.

[161] Ng, Andrew Y., Jordan, Michael I., and Weiss, Yair. 2001. On spectral clustering: analysis and an algorithm. Pages 849–856 of Dietterich, Thomas G., Becker, Suzanna, and Ghahramani, Zoubin (eds.), *Advances in Neural Information Processing Systems*, vol. 14. Cambridge, MA: Massachusetts Institute of Technology Press.

[162] Ni, Chien-Chun, Lin, Yu-Yao, Luo, Feng, and Gao, Jie. 2019a. Author correction: community detection on networks with Ricci flow. *Scientific Reports*, **9**(12870).

[163] Ni, Chien-Chun, Lin, Yu-Yao, Luo, Feng, and Gao, Jie. 2019b. Community detection on networks with Ricci flow. *Scientific Reports*, **9**(9984).

[164] Olfati-Saber, Reza, and Murray, Richard M. 2004. Consensus problems in networks of agents with switching topology and time-delays. *IEEE Transactions on Automatic Control*, **49**(9), 1520–1533.

[165] Ollivier, Yann. 2009. Ricci curvature of Markov chains on metric spaces. *Journal of Functional Analysis*, **256**(3), 810–864.

[166] Ollivier, Yann. 2010. A survey of Ricci curvature for metric spaces and Markov chains. Pages 343–381 of Kotani, Motoko, Hino, Masanori, and Kumagai, Takashi (eds.), *Probabilistic Approach to Geometry. Advanced Studies in Pure Mathematics*, vol. 57. Mathematical Society of Japan, Tokyo.

[167] Osher, Stanley J., and Sethian, James A. 1988. Fronts propagating with curvature-dependent speed: algorithms based on Hamilton–Jacobi formulations. *Journal of Computational Physics*, **79**(1), 12–49.

[168] Parker, Brian J., and Feng, Dagan D. 2005. Graph-based Mumford–Shah segmentation of dynamic PET with application to input function estimation. *IEEE Transactions on Nuclear Science*, **52**(1), 79–89.

[169] Peng, Richard, Sun, He, and Zanetti, Luca. 2017. Partitioning well-clustered graphs: spectral clustering works! *SIAM Journal on Computing*, **46**(2), 710–743.

[170] Peres, Yuval, and Sheffield, Scott. 2008. Tug-of-war with noise: a game-theoretic view of the p-Laplacian. *Duke Mathematical Journal*, **145**(1), 91–120.

[171] Porter, Mason A., Onnela, Jukka-Pekka, and Mucha, Peter J. 2009. Communities in networks. *Notices of the American Mathematical Society*, **56**(9), 1082–1097, 1164–1166.

[172] Rak, Annie. 2017. *Advection on Graphs*. http://nrs.harvard.edu/urn-3: HUL.InstRepos:38779537. Senior thesis.

[173] Ruuth, Steven J. 1996. Efficient algorithms for diffusion-generated motion by mean curvature. PhD thesis, University of British Columbia.

[174] Schaeffer, Satu Elisa. 2007. Graph clustering. *Computer Science Review*, **1**(1), 27–64.

[175] Shen, Jianhong, and Kang, Sung Ha. 2007. Quantum TV and applications in image processing. *Inverse Problems and Imaging*, **1**(3), 557–575.

[176] Shi, Jianbo, and Malik, Jitendra. 2000. Normalized cuts and image segmentation. *IEEE Transactions on Pattern Analysis and Machine Intelligence*, **22**(8), 888–905.

[177] Shubin, Mikhail A. 1994. Discrete Magnetic Laplacian. *Communications in Mathematical Physics*, **164**, 259–275.

[178] Sinclair, Alistair, and Jerrum, Mark. 1989. Approximate counting, uniform generation and rapidly mixing Markov chains. *Information and Computation*, **82**(1), 93–133.

[179] Slepčev, Dejan, and Thorpe, Matthew. 2019. Analysis of p-Laplacian regularization in semisupervised learning. *SIAM J. Math. Anal.*, **51**(3), 2085–2120.

[180] Smola, Alexander J., and Kondor, Risi. 2003. Kernels and regularization on graphs. Pages 144–158 of Schölkopf, Bernhard, and Warmuth, Manfred K. (eds.), *Learning Theory and Kernel Machines*. Lecture Notes in Computer Science (LNAI), vol. 2777. Berlin: Springer.

[181] Szeliski, Richard, Zabih, Ramin, Scharstein, Daniel, Veksler, Olga, Kolmogorov, Vladimir, Agarwala, Aseem, Tappen, Marshall, and Rother, Carsten. 2008. A comparative study of energy minimization methods for Markov random fields with smoothness-based priors. *IEEE Transactions on Pattern Analysis and Machine Intelligence*, **30**(6), 1068–1080.

[182] Ta, Vinh-Thong, Elmoataz, Abderrahim, and Lézoray, Olivier. 2008. Nonlocal morphological levelings by partial difference equations over weighted graphs. Pages 1–4 of *2008 19th International Conference on Pattern Recognition*. IEEE Computer Society Digital Library. www .computer.org/csdl/proceedings/icpr/2008/12OmNx8wTfL.

[183] Ta, Vinh-Thong, Elmoataz, Abderrahim, and Lézoray, Olivier. 2011. Nonlocal PDEs-based morphology on weighted graphs for image and

data processing. *IEEE Transactions on Image Processing*, **20**(6), 1504–1516.

[184] Thorpe, Matthew, and Wang, Bao. 2022. Robust certification for Laplace learning on geometric graphs. Pages 896–920 of Bruna, Joan, Hesthaven, Jan, and Zdeborova, Lenka (eds.), *Proceedings of the 2nd Mathematical and Scientific Machine Learning Conference*. Proceedings of Machine Learning Research, vol. 145. Brookline, MA: Microtome Publishing.

[185] Tian, Yu, Lubberts, Zachary, and Weber, Melanie. 2023. *Curvature-Based Clustering on Graphs*. arxiv.org/abs/2307.10155v1 [cs.SI].

[186] van der Hoorn, Pim, Cunningham, William J., Lippner, Gabor, Trugenberger, Carlo, and Krioukov, Dmitri. 2021. Ollivier–Ricci curvature convergence in random geometric graphs. *Physical Review Research*, **3**(Mar), 013211.

[187] van Gennip, Yves. 2019. Graph MBO on star graphs and regular trees. With corrections to DOI 10.1007/s00032-014-0216-8. *Milan Journal of Mathematics*, **87**(1), 141–168.

[188] van Gennip, Yves. 2020. An MBO scheme for minimizing the graph Ohta–Kawasaki functional. *Journal of Nonlinear Science*, **30**, 2325–2373.

[189] van Gennip, Yves, and Bertozzi, Andrea L. 2012. Γ-convergence of graph Ginzburg–Landau functionals. *Advances in Differential Equations*, **17**(11–12), 1115–1180.

[190] van Gennip, Yves, and Budd, Jeremy. 2024. *Differential Equations and Variational Methods on Graphs: with Applications in Machine Learning and Image Analysis*. Cambridge: Cambridge University Press.

[191] van Gennip, Yves, Guillen, Nestor, Osting, Braxton, and Bertozzi, Andrea L. 2014. Mean curvature, threshold dynamics, and phase field theory on finite graphs. *Milan Journal of Mathematics*, **82**(1), 3–65.

[192] Vol'pert, Aizik Isaakovich. 2015. Differential equations on graphs. *Mathematical Modelling of Natural Phenomena*, **10**(5), 6–15. Reprinted with permission from Mathematics of the USSR-Sbornik, Vol. 17 (1972), no. 4.

[193] von Luxburg, Ulrike. 2007. A tutorial on spectral clustering. *Statistics and Computing*, **17**(4), 395–416.

[194] Wang, Yu-Xiang, Sharpnack, James, Smola, Alexander J., and Tibshirani, Ryan J. 2016. Trend filtering on graphs. *Journal of Machine Learning Research*, **17**(105), 1–41.

[195] Wardetzky, Max, Mathur, Saurabh, Kälberer, Felix, and Grinspun, Eitan. 2007. Discrete Laplace operators: no free lunch. Pages 33–37 of

SGP '07: Proceedings of the Fifth Eurographics Symposium on Geometry Processing. Goslar: Eurographics.

[196] Weber, Melanie, Saucan, Emil, and Jost, Jürgen. 2017a. Characterizing complex networks with Forman–Ricci curvature and associated geometric flows. *Journal of Complex Networks*, **5**(4), 527–550.

[197] Weber, Melanie, Saucan, Emil, and Jost, Jürgen. 2017b. Coarse geometry of evolving networks. *Journal of Complex Networks*, **6**(5), 706–732.

[198] Weihs, Adrien and Thorpe, Matthew. 2024. Consistency of fractional graph-Laplacian regularization in semi-supervised learning with finite labels. *SIAM Journal on Mathematical Analysis*. **56**(4). 4253–4295. https://doi.org/10.1137/23M1559087.

[199] Wigderson, Yuval. 2016. *Harmonic Functions on Graphs*. https://web.stanford.edu/yuvalwig/math/teaching/HarmonicNotes.pdf. Online notes for Mathcamp 2016, Colby College, Waterville, ME; accessed 4 August 2022.

[200] Xia, Feng, Sun, Ke, Yu, Shuo, Aziz, Abdul, Wan, Liangtian, Pan, Shirui, and Liu, Huan. 2021. Graph learning: a survey. *IEEE Transactions on Artificial Intelligence*, **2**(2), 109–127.

[201] Yan, Xiaoran, Teng, Shang-hua, Lerman, Kristina, and Ghosh, Rumi. 2016. Capturing the interplay of dynamics and networks through parameterizations of Laplacian operators. *PeerJ Computer Science*, **2**(e57).

[202] Zhang, Songyang, Ding, Zhi, and Cui, Shuguang. 2020. Introducing hypergraph signal processing: theoretical foundation and practical applications. *IEEE Internet of Things Journal*, **7**(1), 639–660.

[203] Zhao, Yufei. 2015. Hypergraph limits: a regularity approach. *Random Structures & Algorithms*, **47**(2), 205–226.

[204] Zhou, Dengyong, Huang, Jiayuan, and Schölkopf, Bernhard. 2005. Learning from labeled and unlabeled data on a directed graph. Pages 1036–1043 of De Raedt, Luc, and Wrobel, Stefan (eds.), *Proceedings of the 22nd International Conference on Machine Learning*. New York, NY: Association for Computing Machinery.

[205] Zhou, Dengyong, and Schölkopf, Bernhard. 2004 (January). A regularization framework for learning from graph data. Pages 132–137 of *ICML Workshop on Statistical Relational Learning and Its Connections to Other Fields*. Munich: Max Planck Society for the Advancement of Science. https://is.mpg.de/publications/2688.

[206] Zhou, Dengyong, and Schölkopf, Bernhard. 2005. Regularization on discrete spaces. Pages 361–368 of Kropatsch, Walter G., Sablatnig, Robert, and Hanbury, Allan (eds.), *Pattern Recognition*. Berlin: Springer.

[207] Zhou, Dengyong, Schölkopf, Bernhard, and Hofmann, Thomas. 2004. Semi-supervised learning on directed graphs. Pages 1633–1640 of Saul, Lawrence K., Weiss, Yair, and Bottou, Léon (eds.), *Advances in Neural Information Processing Systems (NIPS 2004)*, vol. 17. Cambridge, MA: Masachusetts Institute of Technology Press.

[208] Zhou, Xueyuan, and Belkin, Mikhail. 2011. Semi-supervised learning by higher order regularization. Pages 892–900 of Gordon, Geoffrey, Dunson, David, and Dudík, Miroslav (eds.), *Proceedings of the Fourteenth International Conference on Artificial Intelligence and Statistics*. Proceedings of Machine Learning Research, vol. 15. Fort Lauderdale, FL: PMLR.

[209] Zhu, Rong, Zou, Zhaonian, and Li, Jianzhong. 2017. SimRank on uncertain graphs. *IEEE Transactions on Knowledge and Data Engineering*, **29**(11), 2522–2536.

[210] Zhu, Xiaojin, Lafferty, John, and Ghahramani, Zoubin. 2003a. Combining active learning and semi-supervised learning using Gaussian fields and harmonic functions. Pages 215–222 of *Proceedings of the Twentieth International Conference on Machine Learning (ICLM-2003)*. Washington, DC: Association for the Advancement of Artificial Intelligence.

[211] Zhu, Xiaojin, Ghahramani, Zoubin, and Lafferty, John. 2003b. Semi-supervised learning using Gaussian fields and harmonic functions. Pages 912–919 of Fawcett, Tom, and Mishra, Nina (eds.), *Proceedings of the Twentieth International Conference on Machine Learning (ICLM-2003)*. Washington, DC: Association for the Advancement of Artificial Intelligence.

[212] Zucal, Giulio. 2023. Action convergence of general hypergraphs and tensors. arxiv.org/abs/2308.00226v1 [math.CO].

Acknowledgements

First of all we would like to thank Daniel Tenbrinck for taking the initiative that has made it possible for this work to come into existence. It, and [190], grew from the fertile ground that has been the NoMADS (Nonlocal Methods for Arbitrary Data Sources) project which was funded by the European Union's Horizon 2020 research and innovation programme under the Marie Skłodowska-Curie grant agreement No. 777826.

Our thank also goes out to Luca Calatroni who has been our main point of contact for all questions editorial and David Tranah, our invaluable contact at Cambridge University Press. Furthermore, we very much appreciate the feedback of the two anonymous reviewers, whose comments have led to many improvements throughout this Element.

The content of this Element is built upon the expertise we have built in the course of our own research over many years, as well as the expertise of many others which we have had the privilege to learn from through the literature, scientific presentations, and – most enjoyably – many personal conversations. It would be impossible to thank all the people whose influence can be found to a smaller or larger degree in this Element, so we restrict ourselves to mentioning Andrea Bertozzi at the University of California, Los Angeles, and Abderrahim Elmoataz at the Université de Caen Normandie, and their many collaborators, who through their scientific works and their personal engagement have put the field of PDE-inspired differential equations on graphs for imaging and machine learning on the map as a vital and vibrant area of research. It can always remain a matter of debate in the larger community what may or even should be considered the origin of a new (sub)field in mathematics, but at least in the narrow context of the authors' own contributions to this field, the people and groups from Los Angeles and Caen have been instrumental in shaping it. Moreover, we would like to thank explicitly Jonas Latz for his contributions to our comment on continuous-time Markov chains in Remark 3.5 and Daniele Avitabile for pointing out an alternative name for the semidiscrete implicit Euler scheme (see footnote 63).

Funding Statement

The authors acknowledge financial support by the European Union's Horizon 2020 research and innovation programme under the Marie Skłodowska-Curie grant agreement No. 777826 via the NoMADS project. The second author has received funding from the Deutsche Forschungsgemeinschaft (DFG, German Research Foundation) under Germany's Excellence Strategy - EXC-2047/1 - 390685813, and from start-up funds at the California Institute of Technology.

The open access edition of this Element was financed by the above-mentioned NoMADS project and the TU Delft Open Access Fund.

Cambridge Elements ≡

Non-Local Data Interactions: Foundations and Applications

Series Editor

Luca Calatroni
Centre National de la Recherche Scientifique (CNRS)

Luca Calatroni is a permanent junior research scientist of the French Centre of Scientific Research (CNRS) at the laboratory I3S of Sophia-Antipolis, France. He got his PhD in applied mathematics in 2016 as part of the Cambridge Centre for Analysis (DTC) and he worked as post-doctoral research fellow at the École Polytechnique (Palaiseau, France) with a *Lecteur Hadamard* fellowship funded by the FMJH. His research interests include variational models for mathematical imaging, inverse problems, non-smooth and non-convex optimization with applications to biomedical imaging, computational neurosciences and digital art restoration.

Editorial Board

About the Series

This series provides a mathematical description of the modelling, the analysis and the optimisation aspects of processing data that features complex and non-local relationships. It is intended for both students and researchers wishing to deepen their understanding of non-local analysis and explore applications to image and data processing.

Non-Local Data Interactions: Foundations and Applications

Printed in the United States
by Baker & Taylor Publisher Services